UNLOCK THE CASH IN YOUR BACKYARD

DEVELOP YOUR UNUSED LAND
WITHOUT SPENDING ANY
OF YOUR MONEY

IVA NORRIS

'Iva presents a great case for homeowners to subdivide and develop their own property. No longer do owners need to give up large profits to professional developers – they follow this guide to, as Iva says, unlock the cash in your backyard.'

Justin Kirton – Property Developer and Investor – Melbourne, Australia

'Working for some time with Iva has allowed me to witness first hand her passion for real estate and her deep desire to help people to realise their dreams. This book is a prime example of her sharing her knowledge and experiences to better the lives of many.'

Robin Power – Property Developer and Educator – Melbourne, Australia

'Iva has brilliantly outlined an innovative roadmap for Australian home owners to prosper from her worldly knowledge of real estate investing, to create wealth out of ingenuity in your own backyard.'

David Bernstein – Private Lender and Investor – Atlanta, Georgia

'I have acted for Iva in a number of matters and have without exception found her to be a person of great integrity, flair and creativity. She prides herself on getting the best results for her clients and doing so in a most cost efficient and timely manner.'

Michael J. Pharr – Property and Tax Principal, Rogers & Gaylard Lawyers – Melbourne, Australia

'By reading the step-by-step guide in this book you will know how to select a team which will put you at ease when considering developing your block. Iva has an ability to work with the local councils which produces the best results for her clients. She provides reliable and competent information.

I have watched Iva for some years now as she applies her knowledge both from overseas and here in Australia. The most important thing is when Iva presents the issues and couples them with the right knowledge, people overcome their fear and find it easy to take control of their future. All you have to do when you have finished reading this book is take action.

In this book you will find fascinating stories of homeowners as well as those drawn from Iva's own experiences. It contains Iva's simple recipe for success. If you want to take control of your financial destiny, this book is an absolute must read. I am proud to recommend her book.'

Margaret Nagy – Property Investor – Melbourne, Australia

'I have had the pleasure of counting Iva among my friends for many years. My admiration for her stems from her ability to help others realize dreams through vision, insight, commitment, and tenacity. Add to that a heart that cares about the well-being of people and you have Iva.

Iva's experience and purpose come through in this book; enabling the dream of those who want to improve their lifestyle, in a new home by following her approach to subdivide and develop their land.'

Alfredo Max Säuberlich – A friend forever and ever – Brazil

'Iva is smart, dynamic and active with great vision, delivering positive outcomes to her clients. A woman with whom I partnered for many years – I provided the capital and she with her focus, business acumen and team delivered excellent financial results. Above all that, what counted most was the honesty and trust that was built – a multiple-year track record of profits and no losses, was not a bad thing either!'

Alexandre Radtke – Attorney and Stock Market Investor – Brazil

"When I met Iva, I had no idea that I could use my property to develop without spending any of my money. After I learned about her approach, it was a no-brainer. By doing the joint venture with Iva by getting permits approved for the development of three townhouses, I was able to sell my property for way more than if I had sold it as-is. I couldn't be happier."

Tathra Street and Emma Lynch

First published in 2018 by Grammar Factory

A catalogue record for this book is available from the National Library of Australia

NATIONAL LIBRARY OF AUSTRALIA

Printed in Australia by McPherson's Printing Pty Ltd
Cover design by Designerbility
Cover photography by Laila Chaves
Editing and book production by Grammar Factory

Disclaimer

The material in this publication is of the nature of general comment only, and does not represent professional advice. It is not intended to provide specific guidance for particular circumstances and it should not be relied on as the basis for any decision to take action or not take action on any matter which it covers. Readers should obtain professional advice where appropriate, before making any such decision. To the maximum extent permitted by law, the author and publisher disclaim all responsibility and liability to any person, arising directly or indirectly from any person taking or not taking action based on the information in this publication.

CONTENTS

Iva Norris has been an ambassador of World Vision since 2007, which is committed to eliminating poverty and its causes. The profits of all book sales will be donated to worthy causes.

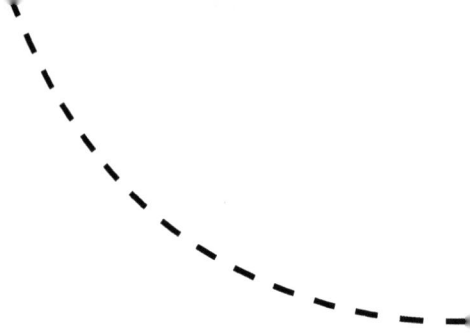

FOREWORD

---------- X

I met Iva when she first came to Australia and it was clear that she had a real passion for property. Keeping in touch over the next following months Iva demonstrated that her strong experience in Brazil and also in the USA was applicable here in Australia. Her passion for helping others who are less fortunate was also a large part of her driving force. That first year saw Iva searching for the best possible way for her to combine her talents and abilities into a business which would fulfil her dreams.

Her integrity, openness and honesty have always been massive beacons for me, she also has the ability to look at potential projects and see other, less obvious, opportunities. The creation of opportunities and the desire to learn everything in support of developing those opportunities are hugely attractive personal and business attributes Iva possesses. Watching her overcome obstacles and create her business framework has been inspiring and in some ways quite humbling.

She clearly wants all parties involved in her developments to have clear goals and objectives. Her passion to assist clients in identifying and meeting those goals is something that she wants to achieve each time, to the degree where, if she cannot do that she will not be involved in the project. Her thinking outside the square assists her and those around her to also achieve the often hackneyed win/win solution.

Iva's desire to inform people of the process to be taken in subdividing and developing their blocks of land has resulted in a book two years in the making. It is a body of work on a subject which does not have only one "right" answer – causing her to present the most likely paths a home owner will take. Although there are undoubtedly other right answers, Iva's approach will serve the majority of Australians seeking to understand property subdivision and development, arming them with the tools necessary to, paraphrasing her 'unlock the value in their backyards'.

John Herniman – Architect

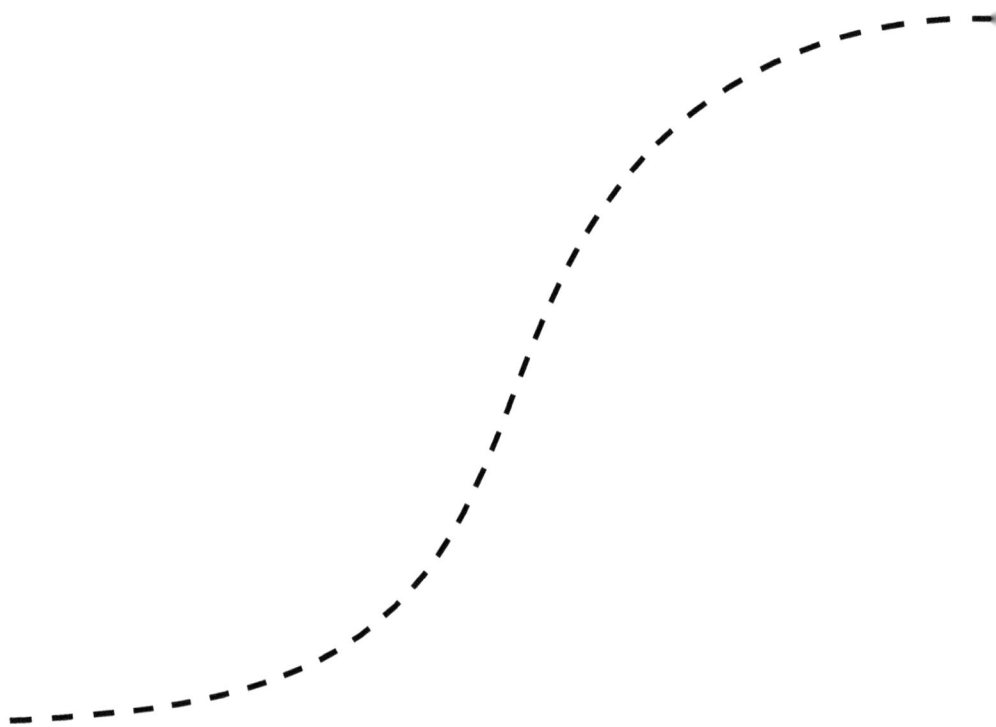

INTRODUCTION: BURIED TREASURE

- - - - - - - - - - - - -**X**

How many times have you examined your financial situation and wondered, 'How do I find enough money to renovate or update my home, or even develop my backyard, so I can pay off my mortgage, afford a holiday or retire earlier?'

Imagine how easy life would be if you won the lottery or found a stash of hidden treasure. You'd be able to afford everything your heart desires, and ensure your family is well taken care of. Imagine paying off your mortgage once and for all, taking that dream holiday you and your spouse have always talked about, or being able to contribute to your grandkids' tuition. It sounds wonderful, doesn't it? Well, I'm here to tell you that it's all within reach – because you're sitting on a gold mine.

That's right. You *can* come up with the money you so desire because there is treasure buried in your backyard.

Think about all that excess land in your backyard that you have no use for anymore, and are tired of maintaining. Why not take advantage of that valuable asset to improve your lifestyle? There is the opportunity to develop that land for a profit, and you don't need to spend huge amounts of money to do so. Or even none of your money if you choose to bring in a joint venture partner. (See 'Do a joint venture' in Step 3.)

Have you ever heard the phrase 'home rich and money poor'? It applies to people all over the country. There are large numbers of people who own very valuable properties, but who lack the cash reserves to maintain, expand or update those properties, preventing them from improving their lifestyle.

Council regulations and town planning requirements make it challenging to understand what is needed to successfully develop a backyard. Financing options further complicate the decision-making process.

Unfortunately, these challenges are deep-rooted in Australia.

For most of Australia's history, the concept of taking an existing block of land – where a residence had already been constructed – and subdividing it was just not realistic, because families needed the backyard for their children. There was also no real need to subdivide it, as there was plenty of land upon which to build single-family homes.

In unusual cases – where existing property owners wanted to build a separate unit on their property, usually for their extended family or elderly relatives – property owners would build granny flats. Granny flats differ from subdivisions in that they are part of a single block of land and are included under the title of that block. However, without having a separate title, a granny flat cannot be sold as a stand-alone property, which limits a homeowner's ability to generate income from their property.

Nowadays, there is a very limited supply of available land to build in close proximity to central business districts. This – along with an increasing population and diminished housing affordability – is why, more recently, subdivision and redevelopment have become the name of the game.

Why you should consider subdivision now

You look around your neighbourhood and see countless new developments and prices of properties skyrocketing. You might think, 'I wish I had money to take advantage of the market trend of development.' But there are four reason why now is the right time to consider subdivision:

1. Council rules and regulations are now favourable – future restrictions on subdivision could change this.

2. ATO rules on superannuation top-up significantly reduce your tax burden – for now.

3. Capital gains tax rules are still generous – there are calls for changes which will increase capital gains taxes on your property.

4. Why wait to fulfil your dreams and make a positive impact to your life? You deserve to benefit now while you can enjoy it.

With the increase in population and the high demand for properties closer to the city, beach and public transport, there is no better time to develop your property than right now.

The truth is, if you already own a property with a big backyard, you are ahead of many.

Why sell your property to developers or builders and let them profit from your accomplishment of buying a house on a big block and in a good area? Why leave the place you've called home for twenty or thirty years and leave the neighbourhood with which you are so familiar? Instead, why not subdivide your land, replacing the original home with two or more properties? This allows you to free up much-needed cash, while remaining in the spot you're so fond of.

'But therein lies the problem,' I hear you say. How do I come up with the money, time and expertise to develop my own land?

It's easier than you think.

Home building and development has been a major industry in this country for many years, and is on the increase. The increase in new housing construction reflects a range of factors, including land supply constraints, affordability considerations, and a desire to reside in close proximity to established amenities and employment centres. The majority of recent construction activity has been located in areas with existing links to transport, infrastructure and services, particularly the inner suburbs of Sydney, Melbourne, Brisbane and, to a lesser degree, Perth.

According to the Australian Bureau of Statistics (ABS), Australia has a home ownership rate of around seventy per cent – one of the highest rates per capita in the world. Added to this, Australia's population continues to grow. According to the ABS, Australia's population grew by 1.6 per cent in 2016, with all states and territories recording positive population growth.

However, the Housing Industry Association (HIA) says housing supply is not keeping pace with the demand from Australia's increasing population. According to the HIA, one million new homes will be needed over the next five years.

Meanwhile, house prices continue to rise. In the last ten years, house prices in Australia have risen seventy-two per cent and, as mentioned in the previous paragraph, demand for housing shows no sign of letting up.

What all this means for you, as an established homeowner, is that there has never been a better time to cash in on your empty backyard. And taking the opportunity to improve your lifestyle by building your dream home is what this book aims to do.

This book presents detailed information for property owners who want to subdivide and develop their land, so they can not only free up much-needed cash for their future but also improve their lifestyle by living in a brand-new home. It reveals the opportunities and pitfalls of subdividing and developing a block of land, and how to leverage what you have while avoiding common mistakes.

I've been in property for more than fifteen years. If you follow the advice outlined in this book, I can help you unlock the cash in your backyard, thereby ensuring financial security for you and your loved ones. In short, I can help you manufacture wealth.

'Do not wait; the time will never be "just right". Start where you stand, and work with whatever tools you may have at your command, and better tools will be found as you go along.'
– Napoleon Hill

A manufacturer of wealth

I started my first company in Brazil at the age of twenty-four, trading telephone lines, and later proceeded to buying and selling stocks. In Brazil at that time, you had to buy stocks of a public telephone company to be able to have a landline installed in your house. By buying the stocks, you were buying the right to use a phone line. The users didn't care about the stocks – they only wanted the phone line. And the stock at that time was worth cents. Later, as these public companies were being prepared for privatisation, I got a list of all the people who had bought a phone line (stockholders). Then I just had to call the stockholders, offer to buy their stocks, and then sell the stocks at the appropriate time in the marketplace. In this scenario everyone wins: The stockholders didn't know they had stocks, which I purchased for cash (a clear generation of wealth for the owner); and I could wait for the eventual privatisation of the telecommunications industry to cash in my investment (a win). By age twenty-eight, I was a millionaire.

When I was thirty-three I married my husband, Tim. We've since adopted two and a half children from Brazil: Sixteen-year-old Christiane and her six-month-old son, Richard (the half!), and Christiane's ten-year-old brother, Victor. At the time, I also had a thirteen-year-old son, Adriano.

Fast-forward to 2001, when Tim's work took us to Atlanta, Georgia. Six months pregnant and wondering what I was going to do professionally, I saw a TV infomercial about how to buy property without using your own money, presented by renowned real estate investor Carleton

H. Sheets. That infomercial – together with the book *Rich Dad Poor Dad* by Robert Kiyosaki and Sharon Lechter – set the course for the rest of my professional life. I was enchanted by the concept of investing in property. So, I bought Carleton's program and, within the next five years, I had bought twenty-eight properties (with none of my own money). I was buying properties from homeowners who didn't have any equity in their homes and couldn't afford to pay their loan. The vendor won, as I was taking over their loan and thereby permitting them to avoid defaulting on their obligations and ruining their credit record. I was in turn selling these properties to first-time home buyers who didn't qualify for conventional mortgage loans and/or didn't have the ten to twenty per cent for the deposit. By buying from me they didn't need a perfect credit record and they only had to come up with a five per cent deposit. This generated wealth for the subsequent buyer by permitting them to begin the homeowner process earlier and establish their credit histories. I gained as the sale price was higher than the balance on the mortgage I had assumed.

I sold most of my properties before the global financial crisis hit in 2007 to 2009. That same year, Tim's work at KPMG saw us return to Brazil. It was there that I opened and operated three Award Winners Century 21 real estate agencies and started to develop land. I would buy properties in bulk and sell them off individually, financing personally the transactions over multiple years. I sold these blocks of land to individuals with little money down and payments spread out over five to seven years. This generated wealth for the buyers who could not buy in a conventional manner (banks in Brazil will not finance the purchase of land) and who were then the beneficiaries of subsequent increases in land values. I had just enough time in Brazil to develop my formula for land development before KPMG moved us to Melbourne in 2013. Australia is our last stop, as Tim retired from KPMG in 2015. It only took two years but we fell in love with this country down under and decided to stay permanently. So, I sold my agencies in Brazil, kept the passive land development business, and relocated our home to Melbourne, wondering how to leverage my wealth of real estate experience in this new land.

After two years of studying and working in various facets of property investment in Australia, I came to the conclusion that the property investment model of 'buy low and sell high' – which I had used so successfully in the US and Brazil – could not be replicated due to the high demand and high property prices in Australia. My research showed that the best model for generating wealth through property was in property subdivision and development. While I could buy property without my own money and still make a profit here in Australia, I realised it would be a lot of work and the return would be low and spread over a long time. Throughout my career I learned that 'All that glisters is not gold,' and that making money for the sake of making money was not nearly as fulfilling as helping people to achieve their dreams. Therefore I decided to use the experience and knowledge I had gained to help those people who were land rich and cash poor.

'Success in life is not measured by how much money you make ...
Success is how many people you touched with your life.'
– **Bill Gates**

From 2015 onwards, I began to interview and build my own team of town planners, property developers, architects, building designers, surveyors, solicitors, accountants, builders and real estate agents.

I redefined my professional goal to help Australian homeowners profit from their backyard by adding value to property that was, in many cases, in need of renovation or otherwise distressed. (Examples of distressed properties include those in need of serious repair, or which have no equity. It can also refer to a distressed property owner, who could be dealing with a divorce, sudden unemployment, a death in the family, health issues, and so on.)

This book is about – helping everyday homeowners realise the untapped value of their land by showing them how they can go about developing, subdividing and building two or more new homes on their property. Thereby manufacturing wealth.

For many people, subdivision and property development are completely foreign concepts. They are reluctant to investigate what seems like a lot of work when the easy option is to simply sell the family home. But you could make more money through subdivision and/or development than by simply selling your existing home. Subdivision has the added benefit (should you desire it) of allowing you to stay right where you are; in the very same spot you've called home for however many years or decades. It is not difficult – you just need to ensure that you have a clear plan and the right people helping you.

In this book, I will outline all the necessary steps to cash in on the treasure in your backyard. I will also list the professionals you need and how to engage them, plus a number of other helpful resources to ensure the process is as smooth – and as profitable – as possible.

> *'If you want to go fast, go alone.*
> *If you want to go far, go together.'*
> **– African Proverb**

Three building blocks to financial freedom

This book is divided into three sections.

In **Section 1: The Seven Step guide**, I'll guide you through my seven-step process for turning your backyard into cash. This section includes instructions and checklists for you to follow, in addition to several case studies. These case studies feature the real-life experiences of other homeowners who have been through the process – including each homeowner's successes, setbacks and lessons learned – so that you have a better understanding of the major dos and don'ts when it comes to subdividing and redeveloping your land.

In **Section 2: Meet Your Team**, I introduce you to the professionals who will help you achieve your goal. These professionals have been listed in the order in which you'll need them, although you may utilise some of them throughout the development process.

Section 3: Interviews with the Professionals, is an extension of Section 2, featuring interviews with seven outstanding individuals whose professions you'll need throughout this process.

While Section 1 is presented as a seven-step process, I encourage you to refer to Sections 2 and 3 as you proceed through the steps (I've indicated when you should do this). You will find it much easier to complete the process if you approach it this way.

At the end of the book, you will find a glossary of terms, and website links for additional information and insights.

Are you ready to get started?

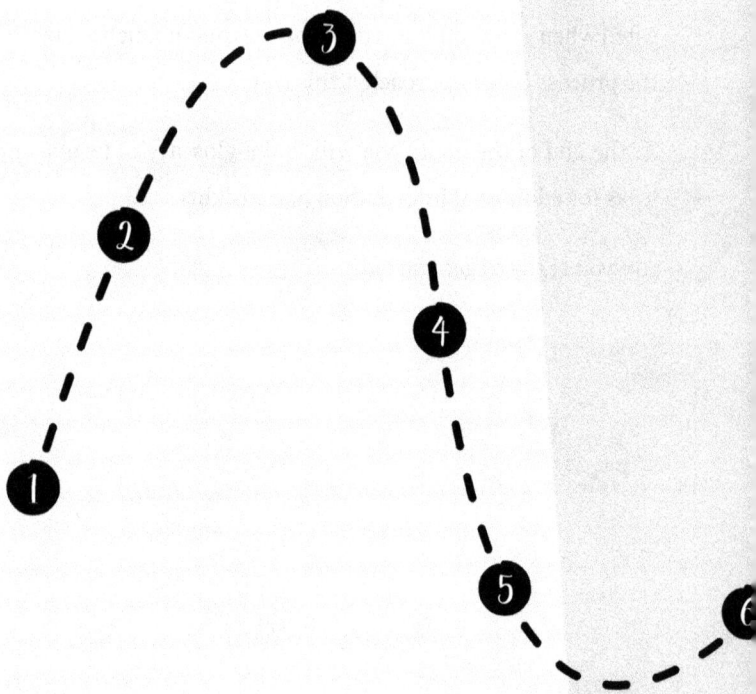

THE
SEVEN STEP
GUIDE

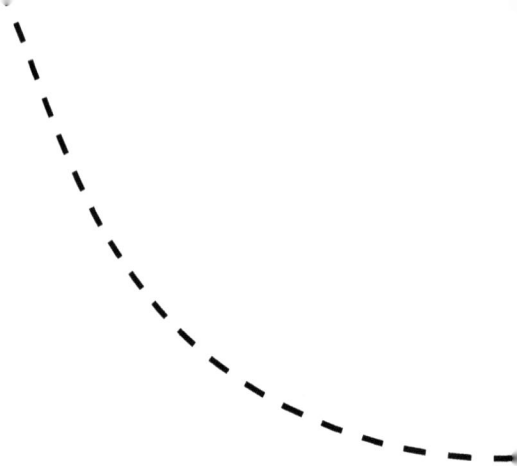

STEP 1: DEFINE YOUR STRATEGY

--------- -X

When you make the decision to subdivide and develop your property, there is so much to consider that it can be difficult to know where to start. The process can quickly overwhelm you, which is why you need to be clear on your strategy before you do anything else.

It's important to define your strategy from the very beginning so you know which steps you'll need to complete, the professionals you'll need to engage, and the time and money required to make it all happen. If you don't have a plan in place, you might have to sell your land at a discount to meet obligations you didn't account for, like paying the architect, interest on money borrowed, and so on.

In this chapter, I'll help you figure out your end goal, determine whether your land is suitable for subdivision and development, help you discover your development options, and offer guidance on the various exit strategies available to you.

Know your end goal

The first step of any journey is figuring out where you want to go. Just imagine if you hopped into the car with no clear destination in mind

– you could drive for hours, or even days, but you have no idea where you might end up.

On one hand, this could be an exciting adventure. On the other, there's a big risk that something could go wrong. Because you didn't have a destination in mind, you could go far out of your way. Because you didn't know how long you'd be driving, you might run out of fuel on the road. You might have left your wallet at home, because you were unprepared. And your phone might run out of battery, meaning you can't call anyone for help.

If you know where you're going, you are far more likely to get there (and you'll probably do it much quicker, with far fewer hiccups and dramas).

The same can be said for unlocking the cash in your backyard. By subdividing and developing your property, what are you hoping to achieve? What is your end goal?

Would you like to improve your lifestyle?

Would you like to increase the overall value of your property?

Would you like to create rental income to help pay for your retirement?

Would you like a lump sum to pay off the mortgage and other debts?

Or would you like the money to fund a new car, a new business, school fees for your grandchildren, travel, or other investments?

Would you like to help your children buy their first homes?

Take a few moments to think about why you're considering subdividing and developing your property. Here are some questions to ask yourself:

- Do you want to generate an ongoing income, or a lump sum?

- How soon would you like your investment to pay off?

- Do you want to stay in your current home, or are you comfortable moving as part of the process?

- Do you want to live in a brand-new or newly renovated house?

- Can you subdivide and develop your property yourself, or do you need a money partner?

answers to these questions will then affect your development choices.

'All you need is the plan, the road map,
and the courage to press on to your destination.'
– Earl Nightingale

WILL YOUR PENSION BE AFFECTED?

Another important question to ask relates to the age pension. If you're on a full, part or transitional-rate pension, will it be affected if you decide to subdivide and develop your property?

Under the current Age Pension assets test, the asset value of an individual affects his or her eligibility for the age pension, and the amount of pension he or she can get. The value of your assets is what you'd get if you sold them at market value minus the debt secured against them (if any).

These assets include items and/or properties that you or your spouse own jointly or in full. This includes properties that are not your principal home.

In most cases, developing your property should not affect your pension, especially if you keep one property to live in (as your principal residence is currently exempt from the assets test).

Is my land a match?

You now have a destination in mind. The next question is, how are you going to get there?

This is when you start crafting a plan – learning what's possible and making some early decisions about your development approach. And it starts with the three Ls: location, lot size, and local trends.

1. LOCATION

As the saying goes, property is all about location, location, location!

How do you define a good location? Well, generally it is where your land is close to infrastructure like public transport, shops, restaurants, hospitals, universities, good schools, lakes and parks. If it is also close to a beach or river, even better.

Why is this important? People are always looking for an easier way of living. If they have everything at their fingertips, they don't have to commute too far.

Of course, it is better to develop in an area that is growing. Where there is growth there is demand, and the highest demand is in areas with more infrastructure.

2. LOT SIZE

The size of your land will affect its development potential. Is it large enough to subdivide while meeting your council's rules and regulations?

Your council will have a minimum size that a block of land needs to be when subdivided, and you also need to consider the maximum area allowed for your land

Corner lots are always the best to deal with; you have two front roads, which gives you more space to work with and makes it a lot easier to maximise the potential of the project. Even better if the corner lot has a laneway – the combination of a corner lot with a laneway can make your project very profitable. The reason is that you don't have to have big setbacks, as you don't have neighbours worried about overshadowing or overlooking. For example, let's say a $500m^2$ lot, in between two houses, allows for only two units of $160m^2$ each. If the same $500m^2$ lot was on a corner, with a laneway, you could build three slightly smaller units of $135m^2$ each. Another advantage is the parking – you have three roads to come up with the best parking option for your project.

Additionally, you have to take into consideration council requirements regarding neighbourhood character and the open space required for each lot. This, combined with the market trends in the area (the number of rooms and average unit sizes), will make it easier to determine the ideal lot size you need for your subdivision.

YOUR LAND MIGHT NOT NEED TO BE AS BIG AS YOU THINK

Recently I was door-knocking in Brighton and I met Johna. He was in his early forties, and I introduced myself as a property developer looking for my next project. He told me his block was too small to sub-divide (as he had already checked with the council), but he was interested in selling as he and his partner, Sue, wanted to move to a newer and bigger home.

I could see the potential of his land and so I met with an architect and a building designer, and came up with drawings for two small houses on his 480m² block – the first was 130m² while the second was 150m².

Unfortunately, they didn't appeal to Johna, as he was looking for a house that was at least 180m² in size.

So, I took the drawings to an experienced developer and builder for his advice. He suggested building two dwellings on top of a single base-ment. The result was plans for two separate double-storey homes with four bedrooms each, two bathrooms, a powder room, two living areas, a study, an alfresco area, two car spaces, and a 44m² home the-atre with a bathroom and kitchen. On just 480m² of land, we had cre-ated two units of 230m² each!

We engaged three local agents to give an estimate of the final value of the units, and the lowest of the estimates was a staggering $1.8 mil-lion each. In comparison, Johna's existing home was only valued at $1.35 million.

Unsurprisingly, Johna and Sue were delighted with the result. If they decided to move forward, it meant they didn't have to sell their house and pay about $20,000 in commission and marketing fees (1.5 per cent of $1.35 million), and they didn't have to look for and buy another house and pay about $100,000 in stamp duty (5.5 per cent of $1.8 million).

By developing, the increase in value of their asset would be $450,000, and the savings $120,000. That's a total of $570,000. The joint venture proposal (more on this later) was to build a brand-new home for them in exchange for part of their land, and they didn't need to spend any of their own money.

Who wouldn't want that?

3. LOCAL TRENDS

You need to ensure the features of the property are the ones that are in demand by people looking to buy or rent in your area; this will mean there is strong demand for it.

This information is easy to come by. Just talk to your local property managers and real estate agents. They are in constant touch with renters and buyers, and will know exactly what style of property is most in demand.

For example, one of our clients had a 1,000m^2 corner lot with a laneway, worth $1.45 million. The options to develop were as follows:

- Seven small, three-bedroom units on top of a basement.
- Five large, three-bedroom units spanning a total of 882m².
- Four large, four-bedroom units spanning a total of 800m².
- Keep the existing house with five bedrooms, and build two three-bedroom units at the back of the property.

The seven units could be sold for $4.55 million, the five units for $4.25 million, the four units for $4 million, and the existing house and the two units for $3.1 million.

However, this is where you need to look at the local market trend in the area. In this particular area, there is an oversupply of small units, which was bringing the price of that type of unit down. Looking at the preferred trend in this area, according to local real estate agents, we would be more successful selling four larger units than seven smaller ones. One of the reasons, besides the area's proximity to the city, was that families from more expensive areas were moving to this area because they can get bigger houses for less money.

Having this type of property in the market is just like selling hot bread. More demand with limited supply means prices goes up. Even if you don't know anything about property development, you can figure out this simple rule. The best way to find out what the market is screaming for is to go to realestate.com.au or domain.com.au and select the location of your property, the number of bedrooms for the house or houses you are thinking about building, see how many properties are listed, and then compare against the alternative. It's also worth talking to a local real estate agent, as they can give you specific insights for your area.

Once you've determined that subdivision and development may be suitable for your property, you need to determine your preferred development option. In other words, at what point will you cash in?

'Don't think about the start of the race,
think about the ending.'
– Usain Bolt

Discover your development options

You've done an initial assessment, and things are looking positive. It looks like your block has the potential to be subdivided.

This brings us to the next question: What are your options for realising the value in your backyard?

There are **five main options** to consider, not including selling your property as is: Getting plans and a permit approved for a development of two or more units and then selling it with plans approved; getting plans and permits approved, subdividing the land and selling separate lots without developing; selling your backyard; renovating your existing home and building in the backyard; or demolishing your home and building two or more new houses.

1: Get plans and permit approved for a development of two or more units, then sell it with plans approved.

When you have well-designed drawings and the planning permit approved for developing, your property will increase in value by ten to twenty per cent, sometimes even more, depending on the location, size and existing value of the property. Builders and developers will often pay top dollar for it, as they don't have to wait for plans to be approved and can start building straightway. (See example in Step 3.)

2: Get plan and permit approved, subdivide the land and sell separate lots without developing

The main pro of subdividing and selling the separate lots is that you don't have to worry about the construction process or how you are going to fund the project. Your expenses will be surveyor, architectural, the planning permit application, the subdivision application, demolition, utilities installation, and an open space contribution if you are subdividing into more than two lots (state dependent). Then you will pay for the marketing and agent commission.

The main con of this approach is that, most of the time, you will make more profit when you go through the process of building on the land, rather than just subdividing and selling separate lots. (See example in Step 3.)

While you can decide to sell with plans for someone else to subdivide and develop , or subdivide your land and sell the separate lots, you will maximise the value you receive from your block of land by subdividing it into smaller lots. This includes demolishing the existing house on the property, so all the new lots are vacant. The new lots are registered with council and you can then sell any or all of them as is, or develop them.

Some councils will not allow subdivision without plans for development being approved, so check with your local council first.

3: Sell the backyard

If you wish to keep your existing home, there is the option to subdivide the land (as in the above option) in such a way that your house sits on a smaller parcel of land, and the rest of the backyard is turned into one or more separate properties, which can then be on-sold or developed.

To be able to keep the front house and build in the back, you need to have at least three metres width of driveway down the side of the property (unless of course you are on a corner or have a laneway behind your house).

The advantage of doing this is that most of the time, your property will hold its value. The reason is that buyers place more value on the living space than the lay of the land.

Let's say your property is worth $1 million and sits on 800m^2 of land. You keep the existing property, subdivide the land, and sell the 400m^2 in the back. Your existing property will hold its value even with a smaller land area, and it will potentially be worth even more if you renovate.

How do you determine how much you can sell your backyard for? Look at local newspapers or online to compare sold prices of similar-sized land areas. Talk to two or three local real estate agents to get an estimate. You don't have to be an expert in every aspect of property development as long as you know where to get the information you need.

4: Renovate existing home and build in the backyard

With this option, you first subdivide your land (keeping your existing home on a separate lot), and then apply to council to build properties on the new subdivisions (in some councils, this order will change), as well as taking the opportunity to renovate your existing home.

As above, to be able to keep the front house and build in the back, you need to have at least three metres width of driveway down the side of the property.

Using the previous example, if your land is $800m^2$, by subdividing into two lots and keeping the existing home, you can renovate and develop on the empty land area, and then sell it or keep it as a rental.

The advantage of keeping the existing house is that you don't have to spend a lot of money upfront, and depending on the level of the renovation you do, you can sell for as much as it was worth before the subdivision, sometimes ever more – as most buyers want to move in straightaway, they are prepared to pay top dollar for the convenience. You can, after subdividing, develop the units at the back and then sell one to pay for all or a portion of the construction and keep one as a rental property, or sell all the units and use the money to renovate your home and/or keep some cash. Therefore, depending on the area and the condition of the house, it might make more sense to tear down the house and build new units on the land.

5: Demolish the existing home and build two or more new houses

This option normally maximises the potential profit from your property. By demolishing the existing home, you can subdivide and develop the total land area. You then have the option to build a brand-new dream home for yourself on one of the lots, and sell or develop the other lots. (See example in Section 3.)

It is very important to make the right choice when deciding what to build on your empty land. If you are thinking about building two units, here are the options:

- **Dual occupancy (side-by-side):** This option is ideal if you have enough street frontage (more than twelve metres, and ideally around fifteen metres). The average dimensions needed for a dual occupancy design are fifteen metres wide by forty-two metres deep (if the property is approximately 630m²). Side-by-side will give you more room to construct bigger homes (as the properties will be sharing walls, and usually are mirror image, which also saves on construction costs). Another advantage of side-by-side properties is that the resale value is better, as both houses will have street frontage.

- **Front and back (one property in front of the other):** If you are building two units on one site, you should only build tandem (front and back) if you don't have enough space for side-by-side or if your council will not permit it. Building front and back means the units will be smaller, the cost to build will be higher compared to side by side, and, if an owner's corporation is required, it means less buyer's appeal.

Going all the way to the end of the project is more challenging, but at the same time it's also more profitable. The bigger the risk, the bigger the reward. If you are averse to risk, this option might not be for you, particularly as you will need more money to fund the various construction costs.

Also, the market can move against you, meaning you might need to sell for less than you accounted for, or rent the property out until the market improves. On the other hand, buyers will pay more for a ready-made product they can see and touch. And the market also can move up, helping you get an even bigger profit.

'Every risk is worth taking as long as it's for a good cause, and contributes to a good life.'
– Sir Richard Branson

KNOW WHAT YOU WANT FROM THE OUTSET

Mick and Jan had lived in their family home for over thirty years. It was the house where they had raised their children but, now that their children were all grown up, Mick and Jan realised they no longer needed a six-bedroom house.

At this stage in their lives, it needed too much maintenance, and they knew they could spend over $100,000 renovating it only to end up with a home that still wasn't as good as it should be.

They knew they didn't want to grow old in that house – they wanted a 'comfortable, maintenance-free home'.

While they didn't need to sell, from a financial perspective, they thought that building three new units would be a much better use of the space.

Mick and Jan are in their sixties. They were both working, and needed to get a loan for the construction on their corner block. They wanted to build a nice unit for themselves to live in, and keep two as rental properties for the first year (to save fifty per cent in capital gain tax), then sell one of them to pay down their loan. In the meantime, the rental income would pretty much pay for their mortgage.

They managed to get a residential loan at five per cent for $1 million to do the construction.

Their project took three years from start to finish (one year to get the drawings done and get the development plans approved, one year to find a builder, and one year to build).

Their house at the time was valued at $800,000. They spent $1.3 million to build the three units, going over budget by $300,000 because they didn't pay attention to the extras (things they didn't think about before signing the contract with the builder, like polished timber floor boards, fly screens, and so on). The current value of their block would be $1.3 million (the corner block opposite them recently sold for this price). The value of the units today would be $2.9 million. If they sold they would end up getting $800,000 net profit.

Now they are delighted with their brand-new home, as it has allowed both of them to quit their jobs and enjoy the lifestyle they always dreamed of.

However, they both agree that it's important to know exactly what you want from the outset, and not to change your mind along the way.

'Our experience shows that you have to decide upon everything in advance. If you start putting all of the extras in afterwards, the builder is going to charge you a lot extra. Take photos, get numbers, be prepared about what you want and when you want it, and how much it will cost, because there's a lot of extras along the way that you might not factor in.' – Mick

Know when to cash in

The final piece of your strategy is deciding when you want to cash in. What's your exit strategy?

By determining your goal and exit strategy from the outset, you'll have a clear path going forward. After all, this is a major process you're undertaking, which will greatly impact your future, so you want to make sure you get it right.

When people think of subdividing and developing their property, they typically associate profits with the finished product. That is, a property that has been subdivided and developed from start to finish, with a brand-new house (or houses) ready to sell. But as an established homeowner, that's not the only option available to you.

Some homeowners opt to sell the property before construction is completed to reduce their holding costs and any associated financial risk, while others might sell the land, and others might wait until the property is complete. Here is an overview of the options available to you:

1. Short-term cash out – simply sell your house as is and walk away.
2. Apply for permits and then sell your house with the council-approved plans.
3. Subdivide and sell separate lots.
4. Develop and sell – sell off the plan or sell a ready-to-occupy property.
5. Rent out the developed property for long-term passive income.

Let's say you're considering the fourth strategy – develop and sell (selling 'off the plan' prior to the completion of building). This approach allows you to capitalise on the strong overseas demand for real estate of this type. (This is because current Australian law states that a non-resident without a working visa cannot buy an established property.) So, there is a healthy demand for Australian properties from overseas buyers at this early stage of construction.

However, while this approach might help you reach a new market, and will mean that you can sell earlier, there are some downsides. Normally, when you sell a property off the plan, you pay a higher commission to the real estate agent to sell the properties (around two to four per cent, depending on the price of the unit). In comparison, the commission charged for the sale of an established property is around 1.5 to 2.5 per cent. (Note that, in both cases, the commission is negotiable.)

Consequently, while an off-the-plan sale is indeed an option, sales of this type are typically for a lesser amount than the price you could achieve for selling a fully finished house. While the choice is ultimately yours, if you're looking to maximise your return on a development, the prevailing wisdom is to wait until construction is completed before selling. Again, knowing when to cash in is critical!

Having said that, however, every day that the finished house remains unsold is another day that you are continuing to fund your development and construction costs out of your own pocket, rather than from the sale proceeds. So, it's important to consider what's the better option for you:

- A smaller profit now, with lower expenses, or
- Higher development and construction expenses, with a larger profit once the development is complete.

Also keep in mind that each exit strategy involves different steps, and may require different ownership and taxation structures, so this is where talking to experts can help you get clear on what is right for you *(see Section 2: 'Meet Your Team')*.

Step 1 Checklist

By the end of Step 1, you should have done the following:

- **Clarified your reasons for wanting to subdivide and develop your property, including a goal to work towards.**
- **Determined an exit strategy: The point at which you intend to cash in, and why.**
- **Understood the common mistakes made by homeowners during the subdivision and development process, with an awareness of possible solutions to either avoid or minimise the problems.**

'Our goals can only be reached through a vehicle of a plan, in which we must fervently believe, and upon which we must vigorously act. There is no other route to success.'

– Pablo Picasso

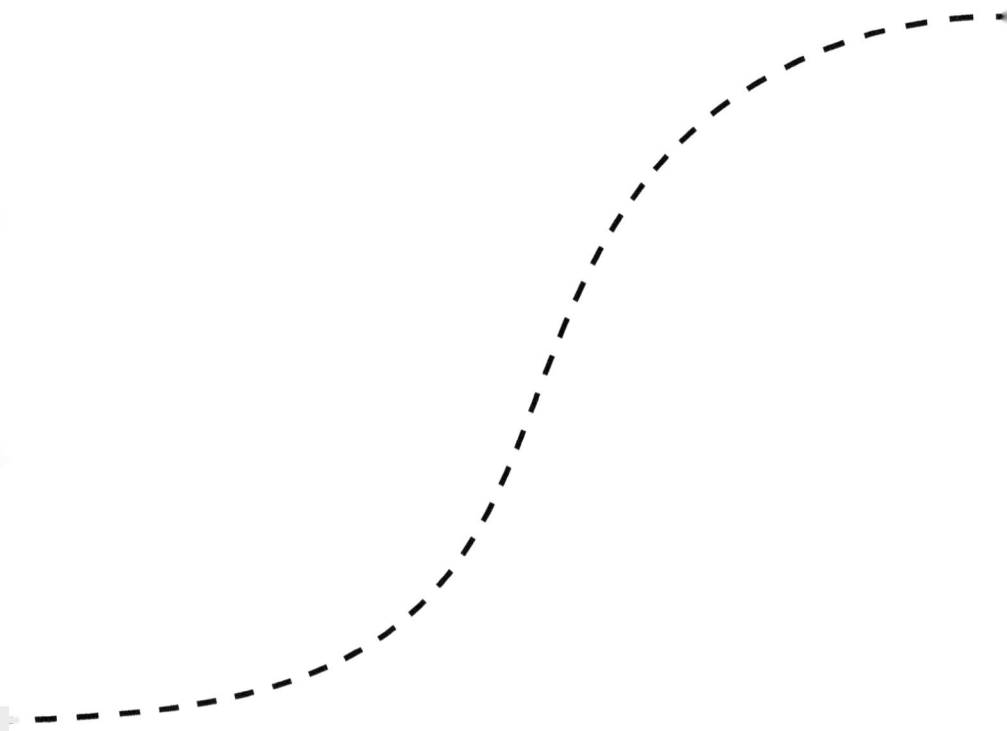

STEP 2: GET COUNCIL BUY-IN

- - - - - - - - - - - -X

When you are planning to subdivide and/or develop your property, you will need to get the permission of your local council before any site work commences. They will give you guidance about what can be built and ensure that the construction complies with neighbourhood characteristics and zoning requirements and, most of all, that it is safe. Without council permission, you can't develop. If you do it without permission, you will not be able to get the certificate of occupancy, making it impossible to sell the property.

Councils must give permission for new structures to be built or a re-design of existing ones. They also oversee any change in zoning, subdivision or development of land. This ensures that any proposed work complies with legal requirements and that other residents are not disadvantaged by the development. So, how can you get your council's buy-in? That's what we'll discuss in this step. I'll show you how to navigate your council's rules and regulations, plus how to get your neighbours on board.

Learn about your council's rules and regulations

As I mentioned at the beginning of this chapter, if you wish to subdivide and/or develop your land, you need to first have permission from your local council to do so. Council permission means that your application has been approved and complies with legal requirements. This information is also needed by future buyers should you decide to sell the land and any dwellings on it.

To get permission and be issued a planning permit, you need to submit an application with supporting documentation.

Every local council should have a website with information regarding the proper submission of development applications, the cost of each application you will need, and will advise of any local, state or federal regulations that need to be followed. If they do not have a web site, you will need to phone or visit in person. Normally, you don't need to schedule a time to see a council representative because they are always available during business hours to speak with people.

Councils also usually have specialist staff, such as a town planner, who can provide feedback on your proposed designs before a formal submission is made. It's important to note that council town planners can't legally act on your behalf. For this, you need a private town planner – an independent professional who advises you, the applicant. Your architect will engage a town planner if necessary. Some architects have an in-house town planner, while others will perform the role themselves. *(See 'Meet Your Team' to learn more about private town planners.)*

After your initial meeting at the council, at which you may or may not ask your architect to attend, your will be armed with the knowledge of what you can do on your property, the next step is to ask your architect to put together a preliminary drawing with elevation before scheduling a pre-application meeting. For the pre-application meeting, ask your your architect to schedule the meeting time with the council and go with you. The council does not charge for either meeting; you will only pay them at the time you lodge your application.

Then, when it is time, you will need to pay for the council advertisement, which is typically a board in front of the house advising that an application has been submitted and that interested parties (such as neighbours) may object if they want to. The council may send a letter to the nearby neighbours advising of your application. The public has fourteen days from the date that the sign is placed on the property to raise concerns and objections.

Before you submit your application, during your viability analysis to determine if you can develop, there are some questions you should ask the council town planner.

CAN YOU SUBDIVIDE?

This is the most important question to ask, as land that can be subdivided offers many more options when it comes to developing and the amount of profit you can make.

If your land has the minimum size required by the council to subdivide, that means you can place two or more units on the existing site under separate titles. If subdivision is not possible, you can still develop as many units as council permits – the land under the units will be common space, with everything on one title. However, this scenario presents challenges when you want to sell individual units.

Whether a block of land can be subdivided depends on a number of things. This includes the size of the block, as each council will have a minimum size at which a property becomes eligible for subdivision, as well as existing features of the block, including powerlines, post boxes, telephone lines or trees that are located unfavourably for the subdivision.

When I first started in development, I went to the council to find out if the land I was purchasing could be subdivided. Unfortunately, there were many mature trees on the site, and the council required that those trees be kept. This created a problem when it came to finding a location for a second dwelling at the back of the property. In addition, there was a tree where the new driveway was designed to be, and the neighbour's trees were encroaching on the boundaries of the site. This meant the new dwelling would have to be set back farther than normal, which could compromise the desired size of the dwelling, which, in turn, would make it difficult to sell.

In the end, I decided to abandon development plans for this site, saving myself the stress and financial strain of trying to sell an undesirable property.

So, start by finding out whether your land can be subdivided. Once you have this information, you can then determine the number of lots your existing site can be divided into, and the nature of the properties that can be built on those lots.

ARE THERE FUTURE PROPOSALS RELATING TO YOUR LAND?

You should also find out if there are any future proposals that may affect the site. (You can sign up to planningalerts.org.au, which is a free service that will alert you of applications near you.)

For example, will there be future expansion of an existing highway, which would increase traffic or make access to the city easier? Any submitted proposals should be studied to determine how they will affect your development – will that be negatively or positively, and how will the timing of such proposals affect you? You may want to speed up your development to get your units to market sooner or, conversely, slow down your project so that any area improvements are already in place when you go to market.

So, make sure you study any submitted proposals, and understand how they might affect your plans.

HOW MANY PROPERTIES CAN YOU BUILD?

As part of your over-the-counter meeting with the council, get information on their design preferences for the number of units per lot. This includes whether you can build side by side or front and back, and if they need to be single-storey or if they can be multi-storey.

Bear in mind, though, that regulations may change. For example, when I was doing research for a prospective joint venture partnership, I went to the local council to express my intention to put two side by side properties on the lot. To my surprise, the council said no, even though a site of the same size in the same street already had side-by-side dwellings built on it.

The town planner explained that while that type of construction had been allowed in the past, a recent change in council regulations meant this type of construction was now forbidden in an effort to preserve the neighbourhood's aesthetic.

So even if you have a preference for a particular type of development, to avoid any unwanted surprises you should always consult with council before you do anything else and spend money on architectural drawings and plans for something that will not be approved.

If your first meeting with the council indicates that you can subdivide and develop your land, engage an architect or building designer to prepare a concept design for your project.

Zoning guidelines will also affect the number and type of properties you can build. And, if you research these in advance, it will help inform you and influence your ideas about your development options. In your initial meeting with the council, they will let you know what zoning your property falls under, and what type of construction you can build. Keep in mind that the council town planners are always conservative with their recommendations. For example, they will often try to allow less density than you are allowed to have. They will also try to control the neighbourhood characteristics and protect the neighbours' privacy.

For example, when we went to council to consult about one of our projects, the council's preference was for a maximum of two units on the site – a double-storey building in the front and a single-storey in the back.

Unfortunately, these recommendations wouldn't result in the best outcome for our project. In fact, the council's version of what should be built made it financially unviable for us to proceed.

The final value for the two units was $850,000 for the one in the front and $650,000 for the one in the back. A total of $1.5 million. With the three units, we could achieve $850,000 for the front one, $750,000 for the middle one, and $550,000 for the back one – a total of $2.15 million. There was a difference of $650,000 in profit – too much money to let go. By understanding what was possible under council regulations, and through a careful consideration of the costs associated with a longer permitting period (caused by our desire for higher density), we decided to move ahead with our original plans.

By following the zoning requirements, we applied for permission to build three units on the site; two double-storeys and a single-storey. It took a year but we got the plans approved for three units.

This project generated a twenty-five per cent return. Sometimes you have to push the envelope with the council to make things happen the way you want them to happen.

Having said that, sometimes it's wise to follow council's advice. For instance, if your application is taking too long, and it's clear to you that they are just taking their time to force you to do what they want, do your numbers. If it's not too much of a loss, accept what the council is proposing. Otherwise, if your application goes to the civil and administrative tribunal, this process could take up to two years and cost $3,000 to $10,000 in legal fees.

Other requirements

In addition to lot size, property type and configuration, the council will have requirements for a number of other aspects of the property. These include:

1: SETBACKS

Any property you build will have 'setback' requirements by council. This is a determination as to how close a building can be to the front, rear and side boundaries of the property. There are also setback rules for any additional buildings, such as garages and sheds.

The distance required will usually be determined by the height of the building at the closest point to the boundary. Your council will provide information on setbacks on its website.

2: EASEMENTS

An easement can be defined as 'a person's right to access or otherwise use a section of land owned by someone else'. The council will consider current easements on the property as well as any new easements your building plan will require. In rare cases, the reason for an easement no longer exists, and you may be asking the council to abandon or set aside the easement.

If you need to make a request for an easement to be placed on the title of a property (for example, to provide driveway access from the street to the unit constructed at the rear of the original block), approach the council to discuss this before submitting your building plans.

The decision as to when an easement will be granted is made by council. The rule of thumb used to determine if an easement is needed is when it serves the common good.

An easement may be granted by council on your property to:

- Allow neighbours road access to their property (also known as 'right of carriageway').

- Grant access to essential services, such as water or electricity, to neighbouring properties.

- Allow access for tradespeople to maintain or repair services on the easement.

3: PUBLIC OPEN SPACE CONTRIBUTION

A person who proposes to subdivide land must make a contribution to the council for public open space. That is, a percentage of the land intended to be used for residential, industrial or commercial purposes, or a percentage (the percentage varies from council to council) of the site value of such land, or a combination of both. (Check with your local council.)

Private open space

Open space is an important component of residential development. Open space includes private gardens, balconies, communal areas and places to dry washing. These spaces provide private places for residents, common areas for neighbours in multi-unit developments, and are used for entertaining, play and relaxation.

Secluded open space

According to one city council in Australia, secluded private open space means any part of private open space or an allotment which is a) screened for at least ninety per cent of its perimeter by a wall, fence or other barrier that is at least 1.5 metres in height and that has no more than twenty-five per cent of its area open; and b) which is primarily intended for outdoor recreation activities. If any of your neighbours have such a space, it must be considered as you develop your plans so that those neighbours are not unduly affected.

Once you have determined whether your idea is viable – given existing council rules and regulations – you should approach your neighbours and get them on board.

GET YOUR NEIGHBOURS ON BOARD

When you apply to subdivide and develop your land, you might encounter objections from the neighbours.

These objections can increase the amount of time it takes for your project to get approved, and can add to your costs. In some councils, an objection will add six months to the time needed to issue a planning permit.

So, before applying for a planning permit, talk to your neighbours and explain what you are thinking about doing. Ask if they have any concerns – they might relate to the new development overlooking or overshadowing their property or yard, a shortage of parking on the street, extra traffic, and so on.

According to the NSW Government's Building Professionals Board, the most common concerns are about complying development, particularly:

- Depth of excavation, basements and retaining walls.
- Height, setback, and number of storeys of a building.
- Boundaries and privacy screens.
- Site conditions such as tree protection and driveway access for neighbours.

Once you understand your neighbours' concerns, try to address each of them as best you can and communicate your changes to your neighbours so that they see you are serious about addressing their concerns. You could even create a table, like the one below, to help you do this.

I've identified some potential concerns and solutions to give you an idea of how you might tackle things.

Concern	Solution
Your neighbours are concerned about noise levels during construction, particularly on weekends.	Generally speaking, it's okay to use power tools between 7am and 7pm. However, timing can differ on weekends and for each state, so check your council's individual noise regulations.
Your neighbours think you're building too close to the boundary of your property.	Check the building regulations with your local council and invest in an up-to-date property survey. Communicate your findings to the neighbour.
Your neighbours are concerned that your new balcony looks directly over their pool area.	Think about the repercussions of your extension while in the planning stages, and approach your neighbour before they read about it on the site notice in your front yard. Consider frosted glass in windows that overlook.

Make sure you work with your neighbours and try to come up with solutions to their concerns. It is very important that your neighbours are supportive of your development. This will help avoid – or at least minimise – objections.

Once you've consulted your neighbours, and have done as much as you can to ease their concerns, you can apply for a planning permit. Please refer to Step 5 for more information about the application process.

Step 2 Checklist

By the end of Step 2, you should have done the following:

- Spoken to the town planner at your local council to find out the zoning of your property and the requirements for subdivision.

- Checked to see if there are any power lines, post boxes, telephone lines or trees located unfavourably for the project.

- Checked to see if there are any current or future proposals lodged with council that may affect your site.

- Learned the council's design preferences for the number of units allowed for your site, and whether you can build side by side or front and back, and single- or multi-storey.

- Learned if there are any open space contributions or easements required.

- Spoken to your neighbours to advise them of your plans and, ideally, gained their approval.

> *'The single biggest problem in communication*
> *is the illusion that it has taken place.'*
> **– George Bernard Shaw**

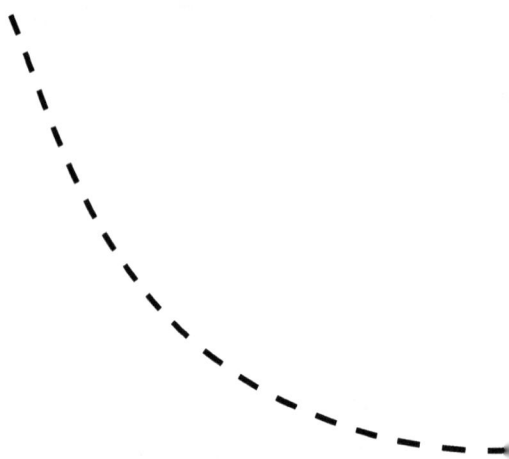

STEP 3: ASSESS YOUR PROJECT'S VIABILITY

In Step 1, you started to consider your options for subdividing and developing your property. Step 2 focused on whether your land qualified for subdivision and development. If your land passed that test, the next step is to determine whether the project is viable.

Remember that if you fail to plan, you plan to fail. This step is critical to the success of your project, as if it is not done correctly, you are indeed setting yourself up for failure. Imagine if you did all the architectural drawings, paid for a surveyor, and submitted your application to the council. You don't want to find yourself having to sell your project before it's finished because you ran out of money, or struggle to sell the units for the price you expected. So, take your time, go over the numbers, and confirm them with a development expert.

In this step, I'll show you how to document your costs (land value, professional fees, permitting costs, demolition costs, construction costs, marketing and sales/rental costs, and so on) and offset them by documenting the value to be received. In other words, the sale price or rental income. In this step, you'll consult with experts in each of the cost and value categories listed above to get the best estimates you possibly can.

Let me explain why this is so important, using a real-life example. I have a friend who bought a piece of land to develop two units. After just five minutes of asking the right questions, I identified that she would make no profit at all on a $550,000 investment (and might even take a loss) in the twelve months it would take to complete. Ouch.

Here are the questions I asked, along with her answers:

How much did you pay for the land? $200,000 (She subdivided it into two lots.)

What was the estimated construction cost and all other expenses to build the two units? $350,000 (Total expenses $550,000.)

How much can you sell the units for? $275,000 each. (However, the first unit sold for only $250,000, so her loss so far is $25,000. If she sells the other unit for $250,000, her loss will be $50,000.) Projected sale revenue: $500,000.

Undergoing a similar exercise will help you look at your project objectively. As well as giving you an indication of the timeline, cost and potential return of the project, it will allow you to identify financial risks the project may present and how they can be overcome.

Here are some of the potential risks involved:

- You borrow money for the project and, after selling, you don't have enough money to pay the bank back.

- For some reason, you are not able to sell the units because it is not the ideal product or is not right for the area. For example, you built a two-bedroom unit in an area populated by big families, or a four-bedroom unit in a student area.

- Your plans are not approved for what you thought you could build – therefore anticipated sales revenue will not appear.

- There is a major construction site close to your property that will take years to complete. Therefore, your site will be affected by noise and traffic problems, which will reduce demand and potentially drive your price lower.

- There is an easement on your land that prevents you from developing. Result – no sales revenue.

- Your property is heritage protected, which means you will not be able to modify the façade of your property and council will look very carefully at your application, even if you have plenty of land in the back to develop. This is highly likely to drive up the cost of construction.

- Your land might have a vegetation overlay, which means you can't remove the vegetation on your land. Therefore, you may not be able to develop.

- There is a development overlay, which allows only one unit per lot.

What do you need to consider? In this stage, the main question you need to answer is: Based on the architecture drawings and budget, does my project appear to be viable? To answer this question, you need to consider the design of your project, the cost of the construction, your exit strategy, and the likely return on your investment based on current market activity.

Note that this is not an easy task, and you will need to allow about two to four weeks to come up with all the costs in order to do the proper due diligence. If you have any doubts about your knowledge, experience, or availability to perform such a detailed assessment, another option is contracting an architect, a project manager or a developer to take care of all the details for you. You can use my feasibility study template at the end of this chapter as a guide to what costs to capture.

Create a concept design

The first step in determining project costs is creating a concept design to minimise the level of effort and costs until your project is shown to be viable. If you decide not to go ahead after all, you don't want to be too out-of-pocket. If the viability of your project is doubtful at this level, you should put the project on hold and wait for conditions to improve.

First, you need to decide which development option you want to pursue. As I shared in Step 1, the five development options are:

1. Get plans and permit approved for a development of two or more units, then sell.

2. Get plans and permit approved, subdivide and sell separate lots without developing.

3. Sell the backyard.

4. Renovate the existing home and build in the backyard.

5. Demolish the existing home and build two or more new houses.

Which option you choose will depend on your personal preferences, the amount of capital you have to begin with (as building a new property or renovating has a higher upfront cost than simply selling your backyard), and council regulations regarding the number and types of residences the council would allow to be built on your block.

Your choice should also be informed by what is selling well for that area. You should speak to several local real estate agents about this, as they will be able to offer their thoughts on the saleability of your various design options, such as the buyers' preference for two townhouses side by side without the constraints of shared driveways, which is the characteristic of a tandem (front and back) arrangement. This creates the need for an owners' corporation, which can lower demand.

Using those factors as a starting point, narrow the options down to one alternative and then develop a list of requirements. If you are building a new property, for example, these specifications may include:

- The number of bedrooms.
- The number of bathrooms.
- The number of living areas.
- Whether the property will have a garage or carport, and the number of cars it can accommodate.
- Whether the building will be single-storey or multi-storey.
- An alfresco area in the back of the house, extending from the kitchen or living room.
- Walk-in wardrobes.

- Spacious laundry room.
- Bathtub in at least one of the bathrooms.
- An open area close to the bedrooms on the upper floor.

Once you have clarified your specifications, I'd recommend engaging an architect or building designer to create conceptual drawings, which will help in the development of your cost and revenue budget. (See 'Meet Your Team' for more information on working with these professionals.)

The architect/building designer will create concept drawings to be used as you discuss your plans with the council, and then will create architectural drawings when you actually submit your application for a planning permit.

If the initial feedback from the council is positive, and initial cost estimates are both within your budget and will yield the return you are expecting, ask your architect to do the architectural drawings and specifications – this will allow you to determine more accurate costings (a builder or project manager will be able to use the detailed plans to create a bill of materials for your entire project). Those same plans are used to apply for the planning permit. This should take your architect around three weeks.

WHY YOU SHOULD CONSIDER A PREFABRICATED HOME

When you make the decision to develop your land, you're faced with countless choices, including: Should you go for a traditional home or a prefabricated home?

Traditional or conventional houses are constructed from scratch, or piece by piece, on site. Their foundations, built from the ground, consist of concrete slabs, pilings, piers, and so on. Skilled construction workers provide the manpower to complete the traditional home.

On the other hand, prefabricated homes, or modular homes, are pre-constructed in factories. These are then transported to the site and set up in sections.

According to Waco Tao, the owner of PowerHouse Homes, a Melbourne prefabricated housing company, there are a number of advantages to a prefab home. These include:

- **Cost:** At PowerHouse Homes, their prefabricated homes can save at least twenty per cent of the conventional build cost. For a 140m², three-bedroom, three-bathroom home, for example, the average cost is $160,000. To build a conventional home, it would be $215,000.

- Construction times: An average house will take about six to eight months, if you're building conventionally. When it comes to pre-fab homes, the same house could be completed in as little as two and a half months. This means homeowners and renters can move in faster, and you can get a faster return on your investment.

- Quality: Prefab packages feature all of the inclusions of a conventionally constructed home – such as kitchen, bathroom and laundry fit-outs, and utility connections – and often include some extras, like better acoustics and thermal protection.

- Sustainability: On any construction site, there is always a lot of waste and rubbish. When a home is prebuilt in a factory, many unused materials can get used on the next project instead. Additionally, many of these companies use products or materials that are recyclable and reusable.

When it comes to the process itself, it is quite similar to building a conventionally constructed home – the main difference being that the home itself is constructed offsite and then assembled on your land by skilled professionals.

When you engage a builder to build a home conventionally, the builder may be required to provide (or may voluntarily provide) a warranty insurance to protect you against structural and non-structural defects and insolvency. When it comes to prefab homes, you will have an agreement with the prefab company (supplier) in terms of cost, but you will still sign a contract with a builder, including the insurance and warranty, to construct the home on site. The prefab company is simply a supplier to the project.

The building methodology has very little to do with local council applications and approvals. However, the building surveyor has to understand the process and materials used, so there are no surprises once the home has been built. It's important to involve the building surveyor in the early days, as they will issue the certificate for occupancy. (This signifies that a building surveyor is satisfied that the completed building work complies with building regulations and is suitable for occupation.)

However, one challenge with prefabricated housing might be financing. The four big banks in Australia are very conservative, which means they are often not supportive of prefab construction. If you want to take advantage of the savings in time and cost of a prefab construction, another financing option is to get a line of credit on your home to pay for the deposit (which is about forty per cent upfront) and the rest when the house is delivered.

When it comes to paying builders and other contractors, they all follow the same standards as in conventional construction, so your payment terms would be exactly the same as in a conventional construction project, with the difference being that the build is completed faster and at a lower overall cost.

Define your budget

Once you have the architectural drawings, the next thing you will need to do is get some cost estimates from a builder.

Use the architectural drawings prepared by your architect or building designer to create a bill of materials (see Appendix B). This is a list of all the materials that will go into your project, from the concrete foundation to the grass and flowers of the finished landscaping – you may need an interior designer and a landscaper to help you assess this upfront. You can then provide the bill of materials to various suppliers to determine costs. The feedback you get from the architect, project manager and/or quantity surveyor can also help you decide from which suppliers to buy your material.

This materials list, combined with the drawings themselves, will be enough for an experienced builder to assign a cost per square metre to your project. Note that this cost will be based on the quality of the finishing touches you desire. This includes the type of flooring to be used, the type of appliances to be installed, roofing material, any specialty labour, and so on. Their estimates will also include their margin on the project.

When selecting a builder for the work, ensure anyone providing a quote is quoting the same scope of work. There is no point choosing a builder who provides a cheaper quote only to discover that they didn't include all fixtures and fittings in their initial estimate, or they were choosing products of a different quality from what you want – this will just lead to increased costs and delays down the track. You want each quote to have the same list of inclusions (fixtures and fittings, flooring, fencing, landscaping, and so on), so you can make a direct comparison between different builders.

For items that can vary in cost and quality (such as carpet or tiles), it is a good idea to include a provisional cost as part of the quote. A provisional cost nominates an anticipated cost (for example, fifty dollars per square metre for carpets), and it is this figure that all quotes will use when estimating a cost for that item.

Why include a buffer in your cost estimate?

Cost overruns (variations) are unpleasant surprises that normally reflect a lack of completeness or accuracy in choosing the finishing materials, or changing decisions after the start of construction. They therefore go hand in hand with builder variations (work that is added or deleted from the original scope of work of a contract), which are more expensive the later in your project they come up. In the trade, these are called 'extras'.

Remember, what you are accomplishing here is determining if your project would be financially viable, so the likelihood of variation should be considered and a contingency of five to ten percent of the construction cost should be added to your budget as a buffer against those future changes.

Here are some examples of cost overruns:

- Terrain and ground conditions. Excavation uncovers a natural water spring or a rock.

- Weather conditions. Duration and cost of rental equipment or finance-carrying charges increase when adverse weather delays completion of the project.

- Variations. Variations ultimately add labour to the project, which will increase your costs plus the cost of any unplanned materials.

- Availability of labour.

- Design errors. Design errors happen. If they are caught before construction occurs, correcting them still generates additional costs; however, if they are not caught until after construction, the costs are multiplied.

- Market conditions (availability of resources). Often a result of purchasing of unique materials from outside Australia. A delay in receipt of materials which must go in before the project advances causes increased cost as work is put on hold and the roster is changed to reflect the problem.

- Payment delay. Payment delays from the bank may see your project in trouble in terms of labour actions or lack of material for the labourers to use.

- Poor project management. The wrong decision on when work should be done or what supplier to use can end up costing the project dearly – imagine the sheetrock installer showing up before the electrician!

To avoid or at least minimise cost overruns and variations, pay close attention to your detailed plans and finishing materials. Consult with experienced advisers (these include Architect/building designers, builders, interior designers, landscapers and quantity surveyors, who you can learn more about in 'Meet Your Team') who can identify where such problems normally pop up and assist you in making the right choices before the first nail is driven or first shovel of dirt is excavated.

The next step is to determine the tax requirements for your project. Yes, this too goes into your project viability calculations. What good is it to make an outstanding return on your project just to turn it all over to the government? If you are prepared and your project is well structured, you can minimise your tax burden significantly.

Determine your tax requirements

Beyond the cost of your proposed design, tax requirements can also have a significant impact on the viability of your project. Your goal when you take on a project like this is to pay the least amount of tax legally possible. So, how can you do that?

First of all, find a knowledgeable accountant who has experience in property development. (See 'Meet Your Team'.) Once you have an accountant on your side, you will be looking at three areas to minimise your taxes – personal income tax, goods and services tax (GST) and capital gains tax (CGT).

If your development strategy involves building and then renting out a new property (or properties), this will also affect your income tax, as that rental income contributes to your overall income. However, you can claim a tax deduction on the interest payable on the original debt as well as depreciation. This will lower the income you make from the home, either leaving you with lower positive cash flow (and less tax to pay), or with a negatively geared property where the interest is higher than the rent – this loss can then be offset against your personal income, and used as a tax deduction.

It's also important to consider whether GST will apply. And, if so, to what extent, and how do you reduce the amount applicable to the lowest possible level? Note that the sale of an existing property does not attract GST. Anyone who buys an established property from its previous owner will not pay GST, as long as that owner is not registered for GST. Therefore, structure the deal such that the sale of any unit falls under this definition to avoid buyer or seller having to pay this tax. Since the buyer pays the GST, eliminating this from sale makes your property more attractive to the buying public. Brand-new properties generally attract GST if sold within five years of building, based on circumstances and initial intentions from the outset.

The other tax area you need to consider is CGT, which is the tax you pay on a capital gain when you sell the property. If you sell a capital asset, such as real estate, you usually make a gain or loss – this is the difference between what it cost you to acquire the asset and what you receive when you dispose of it. The Australian Tax Office provides certain reductions and outright exemptions for sellers, depending on a number of factors.

A few examples will help to explain the above taxes and how to minimise or eliminate them:

SCENARIO 1: TOPPING UP YOUR SUPERANNUATION FUND

From 1 July 2018, people aged sixty-five and over will be able to make a non-concessional (after-tax) contribution of up to $300,000 from the sale of their principal residence into their superannuation fund.

This move is aimed to encourage empty nesters to downsize in order to free up more properties. This contribution will fall outside of existing contribution caps, and both you and your spouse will be able to take advantage of the measure from the sale of the same home.

Imagine that you are sixty-five years old or over, and decide to subdivide and develop your block of land and sell the developed units. The ATO permits a couple to deposit, tax free, a lump sum amount of up to $300,000 each in their superannuation fund. Impact on your net profit? $300,000 times your marginal tax rate. Assuming a minimum rate of thirty per cent, you just saved $90,000!

SCENARIO 2: REDUCING CAPITAL GAINS TAX

Capital gains tax is not a separate tax but an income tax. Treatment of money classified as capital gains income is different from a normal salary or passive income, and depends in certain cases on the nature of the capital asset. For example, at this time, there is no CGT on the sale of your principal residence. For non-principal residences, it depends on the length of time you have held the property and if you bought it before the start of CGT in Australia in 1985.

Imagine you have been living in your current house for at least one year and decide to tear it down and build two units on the same block of land. Your intention is to sell one unit and live in the other. You paid $450,000 for the original house and land. The sale price of the unit to be sold is estimated at $700,000. What is your tax obligation? It depends on how you structured your project, when you subdivide your block, and how the two properties are titled. If your desire is to reduce your capital gains by fifty per cent, you would apply to subdivide as soon as possible, build the two units, sell one at least one year after subdivision, and pay fifty per cent of capital gains, since you are selling an asset held for a minimum of one year.

If you really want to reduce your tax, you can sell the unit you have nominated as your principal residence and move into the second unit for a minimum of one year, before selling it as your principal residence. Remember to allocate a portion of the original purchase price to each subdivided parcel and add in the costs to develop it. This serves to increase the cost basis, thereby reducing the amount on which capital gains is charged.

Another version of this scenario depends on when you bought the house. If you purchased it before September 1985, there is a complete exemption from capital gains. If you bought it after that date, you would need to calculate what that backyard was worth out of the original purchase price, and pay capital gains once it was contracted for sale (not the settlement date).

Below is an example with detailed financial numbers to help you better understand this scenario.

You have owned and lived in a house on a large block of land for one year, and your council will permit you to demolish your original house and build two units on the same block. Your desire was to build two units, sell them, and use the proceeds to retire to another city. How would you calculate your CGT? For the purpose of this exercise, let's say the original home cost $300,000, and demolition and construction costs were allocated at $250,000 for each of the units built. The subdivision was done twelve months before the units sold. Each unit sold for $650,000.

First, calculate what the property cost you. The original purchase price was divided into two components – land value and house value (you can find this on your stamp duty form). At that time, the house value was determined to be $100,000 and the land value equal to $200,000. At time of subdivision, each parcel was assigned a value of $100,000 ($200,000 divided by two). This amount is added to the $250,000 cost of construction to arrive at a cost basis of $350,000 for each unit.

Next, calculate the profit for each unit. Subtract the cost basis for each unit from the sales price to arrive at the profit for each unit. Or subtract the $350,000 cost basis from the sales price of $650,000, yielding $300,000 in profit for each unit.

Calculate the amount subject to capital gains tax by multiplying the profit by the marginal tax rate after any fifty per cent discount if entitled (held more than twelve months) and deemed capital account and not profit enterprise (revenue account). Because you can claim that one unit was your principal residence, there is no CGT on that unit. Because you held the subdivided parcel on the second unit for at least one year, you will pay fifty per cent of CGT unless you choose to realise one capital gains event in one tax year and delay the sale of the second unit until you can claim it as a principal residence, thereby selling both without incurring capital gains tax.

Remember the actual amount of tax paid will be your marginal tax rate multiplied by the capital gain amount. So, the more income you have in any year, the more your marginal tax rate and, by extension, the more taxes you will pay out of your pocket.

Of course, you have to check with your accountant about your tax requirements and capital gain implications. But if you purchased your property before the introduction of capital gains tax on 20 September 1985, you don't have to pay CGT.

Let's say you subdivide your property into two lots and keep the existing house. After subdividing and developing the house on the spare land, you can sell your house tax-free if you live there, and then move to the newly built house. If you stay there for one year, you pay only fifty per cent of the capital gain taxes (always confirm this with your accountant, as the laws change all the time).

A CEDA (Committee for Economic Development of Australia) report, published in August 2017, called for higher capital gains taxes or a reduction in the exemptions. The same report called for tax advantages to be given to homeowners who either sold their backyards or developed their backyard, creating a higher density site. This illustrates why it is so critical to consult with a qualified professional when establishing your tax treatment strategy.

SCENARIO 3: GST REDUCTION

GST is payable upon the sale of a property if you are a developer and have built a property for resale. If this applies to you, then take note because there's also a thing called a margin scheme, which says that if the land a new property has been built on did not have GST applied to it (when purchased), then that margin of GST that would have been payable on that land can come off the GST applicable to the sales price.

Your tax treatment should be captured in your viability worksheet to reflect the true return on your investment from the project and what you do with your profits.

Example: calculating the margin

Jason is registered for GST and is the owner of a property development entity. He buys vacant land from Jacob, who is not registered for GST, for \$100,000 on 20 October 2008. Jason improves the property and sells it to Amanda for \$210,000 on 5 November 2009. Thus, the margin is \$210,000 − \$100,000 = \$110,000. Jason must pay $1/11^{th}$ of the margin, that is, \$10,000, as GST.

Consider your exit strategy – cost and revenue

As discussed in Step 1, there are five potential exit strategies for your project:

- Get plans and permit approved for a development of two or more units, then sell it with plans approved.
- Get plans and permit approved, subdivide and sell separate lots without developing.
- Sell the backyard.
- Renovate the existing home and build in the backyard.
- Demolish the existing home and build two or more new houses.

Each of these strategies entails different costs and revenue levels. At each level, you add value to your block, which drives up the value for your buyer; therefore, one would expect to receive a higher price. However, at each level you also increase the costs involved, so your exit strategy will be informed by your budget and your ability to secure funding (I'll discuss this in more detail in Step 4).

If you do choose to sell a partially complete project, this will require that you demonstrate the potential for additional profits in order to maximise your sale price. For example, even if you decide to sell with plans and permit approved, the project must indicate a certain fifteen to twenty-five per cent return on the project.

The following is an example of a development for the three leading strategies, explaining the cost ramifications of each of these three levels and how it impacts your project's financial viability.

Let's say you have a house which sits on 600m² of land, and you have permission to build two side-by-side double-storey townhouses on it. Here are three different exit strategies you could take, and the cost ramifications of each:

1: Sell your house with the council-approved plans

Every state is different and the cost varies. However, for the purpose of this exercise, let's say the cost for a land surveyor is around $3,000, architectural drawings around $14,000, a town planner, landscape plan and planning permit fees about $3,000, and marketing and commission around $15,000.

Generally, your property with the plan approved will increase in value by ten to twenty per cent, sometimes even more, depending on the location, size and existing value of the property. Let's say your property value today (as is) is $1 million, and it takes six to twelve months to get the plans approved. If you spend $35,000 to get the plans approved, now the property is worth $1.1 million (10% more). If you subtract the $35,000 spent to get the plans approved, the additional profit is $65,000, simply for getting the plans and permit. This is close to a 186% return on your cash investment, which is not bad for a six- to twelve-month period.

2: Get the plans approved, subdivide your land and sell separate lots

In addition to the costs for a land surveyor, architectural drawings, a town planner, planning permit fees, and marketing and commission fees (as outlined in the previous example), this approach also requires you to pay for engineering, a building surveyor, subdivision permit fees, demolition, utilities installation (water, electric and sewers), separate property titles, and so on. Let's say it will cost an extra $50,000.

So your property's starting value is $1 million, and it takes twelve to eighteen months to get the plans and subdivision for two separate lots approved.. You spend a total of $85,000 to get the land subdivided into two separate lots and sell them. The market value of each lot is $650,000 for a total of $1.3 million. Since you've already spent $85,000, the profit is $215,000 after deducting the initial value of $1 million. All this for a return of over 252% per cent.

Compared to option 1, you spend an extra $50,000 and wait three to six extra months to get the land subdivided. Your property is now worth $650,000 for each lot. You will make an additional $150,000 profit over what you made in option 1. The first approach will give you a 185% return ($65,000 profit on an investment of $35,000) and the second will give you a 252% return ($215,000 on an investment of $85,000). This is called cash-on-cash return, as it refers to the return on the money you spent.

But it gets better...

3: Get the plans approved, construct and sell the developed units

Using the same example, property value is still $1 million. You decide to develop and sell two newly built townhouses, with each one selling for $1.25 million. That's a total of $2.5 million.

Now let's say the construction cost and all the other expenses are $1 million. At the end of the project, when the houses are sold, you will walk away from the deal with a $500,000 profit ($2.5 million minus $1 million construction, minus $1 million for the land). That's an extra $500,000 (as opposed to if you just sell your property for its original value of $1 million).

These figures are not taking into consideration taxes, as it is different for each individual/project.

The timeframe, along with the number of units that are allowed to be built, will vary from council to council. In this case, for two units side by side, it generally takes fifteen to eighteen months from getting the planning permit, to developing and selling or renting the units.

At the end of the day, it doesn't matter which stage you decide to cash in. Any of these three options will leave you with more money than if you simply sell your property.

The following table provides an overview of each strategy with regard to the value added, and the most likely buyers.

Strategy	Value add	Buyer
Sell block as is	None unless home is demolished	Owner occupant, investor, developer
Sell block with plans and permit approved	Approved plans and permits	Developer, builders, investors
Sell subdivided lots	Subdivision approved	Investors, developers, builders, owner occupant
Sell or rent finished units	Construction completed	Tenant, owner occupant, investor

You can also refer to the following overviews to come up with an approximate timeline for the project (this will vary depending on which strategy you choose). This will help you to understand when and for how long you might need financing.

Vision, concept and feasibility

Site inspection: One to two weeks

Project finance (finance application): Three to six weeks

Site feasibility and end value: Two to four weeks

Planning and approvals

Land survey: Two to three weeks

Architectural design, scheme and cost estimate: Three weeks

Preparation of other application documentation and lodgement: Four weeks

Planning permits approval: Five to fifteen months

Construction

Appoint builder, project manager, contractors, contract signing: Four to six weeks

Construction drawings and costings, application for construction permit and approval: Six to eight weeks

Complete construction: Twelve months

Completion

Staging: Two weeks

Lease or sell: Six to eight weeks

Total length of the project: Eighteen to twenty-four months

Feasibility:

This is the most critical step of your project, this will give you a clear idea if your project is viable, in a spreadsheet you will combine all the costs related to you project, from the value of your property as is, the value of the units to be build, town planning costs, construction cost, contingencies, legal fees, interest, project management fee, taxes, interest rates to the marketing and sales cost.

For an example of how a feasibility study should look, see the study at the end of this step. Additional comments on revenue and cost evaluation for the construction of two units can also be found there. For an expanded list of items you should consider in your feasibility study see Appendix A.

Calculate your ROI

Now that you have a clear understanding of the costs involved in your project, the final step to determining whether your project is viable is to calculate your return on investment. In order to do this, you need to estimate:

1. The sale price of your property as is.
2. The sale price of the block of land with plans and permit approved.
3. The sale price of the subdivided lots.
4. The sale price of the residences to be built.

To find out that, check the major real estate websites – domain.com.au and realestate.com.au – to see what is being offered in the market. Always look for the homes that are the most comparable to your house/houses to be constructed (same location, same number of bedrooms, bathrooms, and so on) or site (same geographic area and land size). You should also consult your local real estate experts for their input. (See the information about real estate agents in 'Meet Your Team'.)

With the right approach, this input is gladly given by agents, who want to see more inventory for sale and to have the inside track on representing you when you decide to sell. You should come away from this exercise with an understanding of the current value of your house and the (approximate) end values at each of your exit points, as well as the beginning of a relationship with local agents which will serve you well when you actually sell.

Risks

Keep in mind that the market value for your property or proposed development can change due to a number of factors. These include the number of properties in the market at any one time, changes to your area that make it more desirable (such as new transport or new shopping precincts or sporting facilities), and even council limits around the number or size of residences that can be built on your block.

For example, when you apply for planning and permits to develop your land (a process that may take up to twelve months), you can then re-check the market to see if it still makes sense to proceed with the construction or if it is better to get out of the project earlier. Even at this early stage of development you can sell for a higher price, as a developer or builder will be willing to pay a premium because they can start construction straightaway. You also have the option to apply for subdivision and sell after subdivision is approved. This gives you the opportunity to sell the lots individually (subject to local council approval).

Ultimately, if your project isn't viable today, it doesn't mean it won't become viable in a year's time, or that it can become viable with tweaks that lower the estimated cost.

Note: The plans approved give you two years to start construction, or you can apply for an extension for another two years (check this with your local council).

FEASIBILITY WALKTHROUGH

How does this look in practice? Consider the following feasibility calculations using the QwikFeaso tool from Developer Network Pty Ltd.

QwikFeaso
Developer Network Pty Ltd
www.developernetwork.com.au

	Income	Expense
Profit	$ 384,315	
% Profit on GRV	14.8%	
% Profit on Costs	17.3%	
Project Duration	16 Months	

	Income	Expense
Purchase Price		-$ 1,000,000
Stamp Duty (If applicable)		-$ 38,025
Finders Fee (if any)		$ -
Legal & Accounting Fees		-$ 5,800
Development Approval		-$ 28,350
Building Approval		-$ 22,600
Renovations & Minor Building Works		$ -
Demolition		-$ 17,875
Civils		-$ 29,270
Site Preparation		-$ 5,000
Plan Sealing & Titles		-$ 2,770
Miscellaneous Costs		$ -
Holding Costs		-$ 8,400
Council Contributions		-$ 28,000
Rental Income	$ -	$ -
Finance Costs		-$ 129,146
Contingency		-$ 50,000
Sales Commission & Marketing		-$ 65,000
GST using Margin Scheme (approx only)		-$ 85,449
Dwellings		
2 * 4 Br Townhouse @ $1,300,000	$ 2,600,000	-$ 700,000
Totals	**$ 2,600,000**	**-$ 2,215,685**

Image provided by Robert Flux

This example (shown on previous page) outlines the figures for the development of two units on one site with a project duration of sixteen months. The total costs of the project were $2,215,685, and the final sale price of the two units was $2,600,000. This makes the profit of the project $384,315.

Let's take a look at the profit – first as a percentage of the gross realised value of the project (GRV), and second as the percentage on costs.

To calculate the profit on GRV, the formula is the project profits divided by the GRV. In this case, this would be:

$$\$384,315 \div \$2,600,000 = 14.8\%$$

To calculate the profit on costs, the formula is the project profits divided by the total development costs. In this case, this would be:

$$\$384,315 \div \$2,215,685 = 17.3\%$$

The second example (shown opposite) is based on owning the property to begin with, in which case you'd use the current market value of the property as the purchase price. The reason for this is that you can only calculate potential profit when you know the value of your property today and the difference developing will make.

The good news is that because this is an existing property, you don't need to pay stamp duty so your financial cost is lower. This then makes the project more profitable.

If we keep all of the other numbers the same, the profit on GRV is 19.2%:

$$\$498,986 \div \$2,600,000 = 19.2\%$$

And the profit on costs is 23.7%:

$$\$498{,}986 \div \$2{,}101{,}014 = 23.7\%$$

QwikFeaso
Developer Network Pty Ltd
www.developernetwork.com.au

Profit	$	498,986
% Profit on GRV		19.2%
% Profit on Costs		23.7%
Project Duration		16 Months

	Income	Expense
Purchase Price		-$ 1,000,000
Stamp Duty (If applicable)		$ -
Finders Fee (if any)		$ -
Legal & Accounting Fees		-$ 5,800
Development Approval		-$ 28,350
Building Approval		-$ 22,600
Renovations & Minor Building Works		$ -
Demolition		-$ 17,875
Civils		-$ 29,270
Site Preparation		-$ 5,000
Plan Sealing & Titles		-$ 2,770
Miscellaneous Costs		$ -
Holding Costs		-$ 8,400
Council Contributions		-$ 28,000
Rental Income	$ -	$ -
Finance Costs		-$ 52,500
Contingency		-$ 50,000
Sales Commission & Marketing		-$ 65,000
GST using Margin Scheme (approx only)		-$ 85,449
Dwellings		
2 * 4 Br Townhouse @ $1,300,000	$ 2,600,000	-$ 700,000
Totals	**$ 2,600,000**	**-$ 2,101,014**

Image provided by Robert Flux

This is one of the reasons why joint ventures work better than if the developers have to purchase the land, as it is easier to make a profit and to secure finance.

Complete your own feasibility walkthrough with QwikFeaso at www. developernetwork.com.au

Step 3 Checklist

By the end of Step 3, you should have done the following:

- Determined your exit strategy.

- Hired an architect or building designer to do a preliminary concept plan of your project, comprising the physical dimensions of the block and any setbacks or easements across your property.

- Conducted research to determine what price your property would be worth in its current state.

- Contacted your local real estate agent to get an idea of the building trends in the area to determine the size and style of the homes that are most in demand, and what price the end product (at each exit point) would sell for.

- Itemised all of your costs for the project (again, for each exit point) and subtracted it from the total profit to be made for that exit point.

- Created an approximate timeline for the total duration of the project.

- Spoken to an accountant to ascertain how the project will affect your tax position, how you can maximise your deductions, and if GST or CGT applies.

- Made a decision about how viable your development would be in terms of the profit returned to you, and if that is enough to meet your requirements.

Once you've assessed your project's viability, taking into account the various costs and expected return, it's time to take care of the finance for your project.

'The risk of a wrong decision is preferable to the terror of indecision.'

– Maimonides

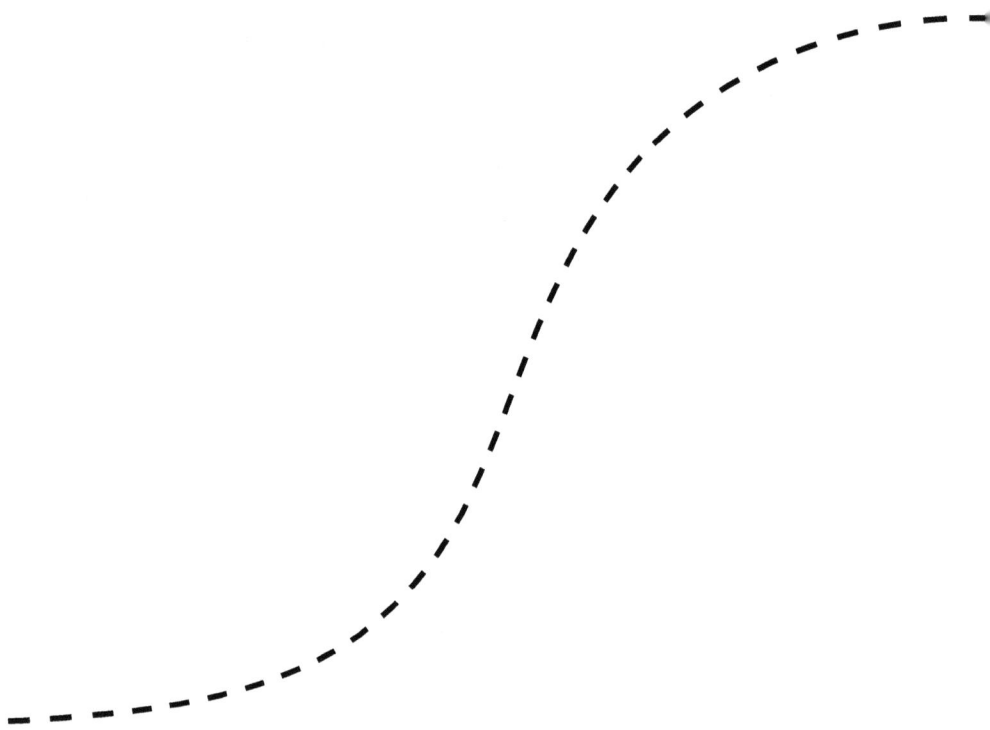

STEP 4: SECURE FUNDING

Once you've assessed your project's viability, taking into account the various costs and expected return, it's time to take care of the finance for your project.

One of the mistakes many new developers make is assuming that they need to fund their development project with their own funds. In reality, there are three options available to you: Getting a loan or a line of credit, using your own cash, or doing a joint venture. Each of these options has pros and cons, which means it's important to choose the right one for you and your situation.

Option 1: Get a loan

Once you have your feasibility study, a breakdown of comparable sales, drawings, and planning approval from council, your first financing option is approaching the bank for a loan or talking to a mortgage broker.

When it comes to home finance, the banks are very competitive. With regard to the big four banks, it is almost impossible to beat their rates. On the other hand, talking to a mortgage broker (see 'Meet Your Team' and 'Interviews with the Professionals') will give you more options in terms of rates and flexibility on the terms of the loan.

If you do decide to get a bank loan, the two most important aspects a bank will look at before lending you money is the equity in your house and the strength of your project. When making an application, ensure the feasibility study for your project demonstrates a profit of at least twenty per cent. Otherwise, it will be difficult to obtain finance.

When it comes to choosing a bank, your current bank may be more open to financing your development project. However, speak with a mortgage broker to find out who is offering the best possible deal and avoid any possible damage to your credit report caused by multiple applications.

The different elements you'll need to consider are the type of loan, the length of the loan (as in, is it short term or long term?), and the interest rate options. These can vary from lender to lender, and, in some cases, are negotiable.

TYPES OF LOANS

There are three types of loans to consider for your development:

1. A **residential construction loan** will cover the cost of two units on the site(there are some lenders who'll do more but these are very few), with separate titles or up to two units on a single title. This lending practice will influence when and how you subdivide your property so that it is looked on most favourably by lenders. In this case, you can borrow against the value of your existing house to finance the project. The interest rate on this loan is the same as when you purchase a home – from four to five per cent – and the rate can be fixed or variable (I'll share some more on this shortly). Under this financing scenario you will start to repay the loan

immediately. While the need for cash flow to do this is important, it is still a cheaper means of project financing than a commercial development or construction loan.

2. A **commercial loan** or **development finance** (construction loan) may be needed when you build more than three units on the site. (The number of units being built will heavily influence the classification of the loan and the requirements for obtaining each type of financing.) While the cost of getting this type of financing is higher, the interest charges can be capitalised into the loan amount so that there are no payments during construction. A construction loan is paid out by the lender to the builder in instalments upon completion of various stages of the project.

3. These are the characteristics of commercial loan:

    *   Loan origination fees are often two per cent or more plus GST.
    *   You will also pay at least one per cent of the construction costs to get your project valued.
    *   You will pay for the building surveyor. Cost is between $250 and $700 per inspection.
    *   Interest rates for this type of finance run from six to ten per cent.
    *   The lender will expect a lower loan-to-value ratio (65 to 75%).
    *   Lender may also require qualified (real) pre-sales.

4. **Private financing (solicitor funds).** Someone lends you their own money. All costs are paid by the borrower and interest rates are higher than the commercial/development loans, between nine and fifteen per cent. Duration of the loan is only for the construction

phase and, similar to the commercial lender, the private lender may require pre-sales be made in order to qualify for funding.

5. If you plan on building and occupying one of the residences, and/ or keeping a residence as a rental property, it is best to investigate acquiring a construction loan that transitions to a residential mortgage at the end of the development. This can save you significant origination fees (an upfront fee banks charge to prepare the loan) and potentially reduce the interest you pay.

SHORT OR LONG TERM?

In addition to different loan types, financing can also be short term or long term.

Short-term financing means you get the loan to start the project and it is used to cover development costs (unless the development is sold to a third party). It lasts for the life of the project.

Long-term financing means you get the money to build and, after completion, the loan normally has to be re-assessed given the focus lenders have on responsible lending compliance. Long-term finance is required if you wish to hold the property once it has been completed.

In both cases, it is important to note when the loan repayments commence. Will they commence immediately or at the termination of development? Likewise, it is important to note if the interest charged is based on the total value approved or based upon how much of the loan amount you have utilised (drawn down). You want to pay interest only on the money you need to use.

INTEREST RATES

When structuring your loan, you also have to consider the different types of interest rates.

The two most popular are variable and fixed:

A **variable** interest rate means the rate will fluctuate with the economy and can go up or down. Variable-rate mortgages are the predominant loan type in Australia, due to the low interest-rate environment.

A **fixed** interest rate means the rate is fixed, usually between one and five years, before becoming variable. It is very rare, given the complexity of a construction loan, to obtain fixed-rate financing for the build.

Both loan types have pros and cons. Let's start with variable home loans.

According to the Australian Securities and Investments Commission one of the key benefits of taking out a variable home loan is that you're able to make extra repayments on top of your scheduled instalments with no penalty. This means you may be able to drastically cut down the length of your mortgage, reducing the overall amount of interest you'll need to pay, and ultimately scoring a better return on your long-term investment.

It's also worth noting that interest rates on variable mortgages are tied to the official cash rate, which the Reserve Bank of Australia sets monthly. If the cash rate drops, and your lender passes the changes on to its customers, you'll have less interest to pay off. On the other hand, if the rate goes up, your repayments will increase accordingly.

101

The number one drawback of variable home loans is the level of financial uncertainty associated with them. Because variable home loans are tied to the cash rate, the amount of interest you need to pay is basically determined by wider economic conditions outside your control. This means that your required repayments will probably fluctuate quite significantly over the course of your mortgage. This can make it challenging to set – and stick to – an accurate budget.

So, what are the pros and cons of fixed home loans?

The primary benefit of taking out a fixed-rate home loan is the greater sense of certainty it provides. Under this arrangement, the interest on your mortgage is locked into the rate it was when the loan was first approved, meaning that even if your lender increases the interest rates, your repayments will be unaffected. This makes it a lot easier for you to set an accurate budget.

However, a fixed home loan is less flexible than a variable home loan.

Fixed-rate mortgages typically do not allow you to make extra repayments – or will only allow them in exchange for a hefty fee. This restriction essentially limits the speed at which you can pay off your home loan, which, in some cases, makes it more expensive than a variable alternative.

In addition, if you make adjustments to your loan or sell your home within your mortgage term, you may also have to pay expensive break fees, often to the tune of thousands of dollars.

In summary, the key difference between fixed and variable home loans is the level of certainty. If you want more freedom, and are comfortable with varying interest repayments, a variable mortgage may be the way to go. Alternatively, if you need the ability to set a budget and make mortgage repayments of a consistent amount, a fixed home loan may be a better option.

Option 2: Use your own cash

Using your own cash doesn't mean your cash needs to fund the entire project – you can use your savings as collateral to guarantee borrowed money, which will result in lower interest rates being charged by the lender. Your equity in your property can also be used as collateral to guarantee a loan.

Lenders will provide up to sixty-five per cent and sometimes even seventy-five per cent of the expected end value of the development, or eighty per cent of the market value of your home. Where you pledge cash savings as collateral, lenders will lend up to 100 per cent of that collateral. Of course, you will not be able to touch that cash until the note is paid down or off, or other financing is used to replace that original project funding.

Option 3: Do a joint venture

If you're in a situation where you need expertise or assistance with obtaining finance, a joint venture partnership may be helpful for you to maximise your project's potential.

A development joint venture is created when a developer and a homeowner work together. The developer provides their expertise, team and resources and you, the homeowner, provide the land. As part of the terms of the joint venture, you will make an agreement with the developer as to how the profits will be shared.

You may consider a joint venture if:

- You have no knowledge about subdividing and developing.
- You don't have money, experience or time, all of which the joint venture partner can bring to the table.
- You have no income or is at age limit, therefore do not qualify to service the loan
- You have no desire to manage the day-to-day activities of the project.

A joint venture can take various forms. Here are some examples of the more typical ones:

- The parties agree to keep the existing house and have it renovated in exchange for the opportunity to develop the remaining land. Depending on the size of the land and the complexity of the renovation, the homeowner may also receive cash.

- The parties decide to tear down the existing house and build two or more units in its place. In the case where two homes are built, the homeowner typically gets a brand-new home in exchange for a portion of their land. Depending on the deal, the owner might receive money from the developer or pay money to the developer as part of the deal.

Many of our clients ask, 'Where am I going to live while the houses are being built?' As part of the deal and depending on the profitability of the deal, many joint venture partners will arrange for relocation and pay for rent on behalf of the homeowner while their house is being renovated or built, and later on is reimbursed for the amount paid for rent from the proceeds of the joint venture.

WHY CONSIDER A JOINT VENTURE?

By partnering with a developer, you're able to streamline the process of subdivision and building on a site and, in many instances, complete the project much faster and at a lower cost than if you were to attempt it on your own. Developers also usually have an established network of specialists they involve for each step of buying land and improving it. These specialists would include accountants, architects, engineers, solicitors, surveyors, town planners, builders and real estate agents, all of whom can further streamline the process.

Some other advantages for you as a homeowner include:

- There is no need to pay marketing fees to find a buyer or to pay a commission to a real estate agent.
- There is no need to spend your own money or time renovating or building.
- There is no need to spend money on relocation and rent while the house is being renovated or built.
- You don't need any expertise or specialist knowledge as the developer provides the team.
- There is no need to find a new home (and pay stamp duty on it) as ownership does not change.

It's important to note that you will *not* be at risk of losing your property, as the title remains in your name until the project is completed. Also, to be safe, wait until the last minute to demolish the house – preferably when the finance for the construction is in place (approved).

Usually the JV partner will lodge a caveat on the property to protect his or her interest. This means that in order for the JV partner to spend their own money to invest in your project, they need to have some security.

From the developer's perspective, some advantages include:

- There is no need to spend a large amount of money or borrow from the bank to buy the land/site.

- Cash is available for other development activities.

- There is no rush to build immediately. This allows time to do all the planning needed for the project, rather than rushing to get all the approvals in place because of the carrying costs of using borrowed money.

- There are savings to be had when it comes to such issues as settlement fees, and stamp duty, which help to increase the outcome of the development.

HOW A JOINT VENTURE COULD SUPERCHARGE YOUR PROFIT

John and Paula bought a brand-new home and were ready to place their former home on the market. After explaining to them the benefits of a JV partnership, and after performing a feasibility study, John and Paula decided to partner with my team and me.

Their house was in need of repair, and they didn't want to spend the money to fix it, as they were planning to sell (in this case, they would have had to pay out-of-pocket marketing and commission to a real estate agent). The property they bought was going to take up to one year to be ready.

The value of their home was $650,000. We applied to develop three units valued at $1.8 million. (The council's preference was for two units. It took us an extra six months to get the plans approved for three units, but the extra time was worth the extra profit.)

The total for construction and other costs was estimated at $750,000, leaving a profit of $400,000 to be split between us. Our contribution was funding the initial costs to get plans approved, build and manage the team and the project, and organise finance for the construction, while John and Paula provided the land. They didn't have to spend any money or do anything and, at the end of the project, they would end up with an extra $200,000.

This example is a great one as it demonstrates that circumstances change. John and Paula decided to sell the property with the planning permit approved, changing their original exit strategy. Due to increased demand in their area, their decision to sell will give them an estimated profit of $170,000 at the time of writing – and they didn't even have go through the challenges associated with construction.

With the extra money, their plan is to pay off the mortgage on their new home and go on a holiday.

How to successfully manage a joint venture

The first step of any joint venture is finding a developer to partner with. If you are looking for potential partners, start by speaking with local real estate agents to find out which developers are in your area. Another option is to examine publicly available plans at the local council for the names of companies who have made development applications in your area. You can also search online for investor/developer clubs or organisations.

Once you have a potential partner, the next step is to give the developer information on your house and the land area, your title, and any previous plans you might have from the past. If there have been recent sales of similar developments in your local area, give them that information as well.

You can expect that the joint venture partner will perform their own initial concept design and budget to determine the profit potential of the project. They will also normally fund the permit application process (we'll discuss this in more detail in Step 5). They may also assist you by using their own funds or obtaining construction financing. As they will be investing heavily in your project in terms of time, upfront money and experience, their return is measured in terms of number of units (you keep one and they keep one) or as a percentage of the project's profit (a fifty-fifty split of profits is fairly common).

If you are both happy to go ahead, the next step is drawing up a contract. A joint venture contract or a profit-sharing agreement allows you to subdivide and develop your property by bringing in an experienced partner to provide finance and expertise.

The partner in a joint venture will typically handle all financial aspects of the project (including obtaining loans, if needed) and will oversee all stages of the project, from applications to council to project-managing the build and sales.

In any joint venture, both parties will have an expectation of what they will gain from it. So, it is important to consider the interests of all parties to ensure that the joint venture is set out in such a way that everyone is happy with what they get from it and with the final outcome. This will help ensure the project runs smoothly.

To achieve this, it is important to communicate your expectations clearly to the other parties and gain their agreement. Do you want to sell the new development or hold on to it and rent it out? In turn, you need to find out what the other parties are expecting so you can ensure this is something you can agree to. The final version of what is agreed between you will form the basis of the legal document that outlines the joint venture.

Normally, the JV partner will get written authorisation from you to perform various tasks. This is a legal document that gives the developer permission to act on your behalf. This means the JV partner doesn't have to chase you up every time they need to proceed to the next level of the project. This includes getting plans and permits, hiring consultants, and so on.

Questions to ask regarding a joint venture contract include:

- What are the responsibilities of each party? (These need to be stated very clearly in the agreement.)

- What financial contributions are required at each stage and who is responsible for payment? (Normally the JV partner will be responsible for the out-of-pocket expenses.)

- What parts of the venture will be taxable and who is responsible for payment?

- How will the joint venture be legally structured and who will do this? (Each case is different. If a company needs to be set up, the developer will normally do it, and the homeowner should have their solicitor review it.)

- How are any disputes to be resolved? (Mediation is the best option, as it is much cheaper than hiring a solicitor. When a court requires litigating parties to mediate, it usually has a list of volunteer mediators who will work for free or for a nominal fee. In other cases, where both parties want a professional mediator, you can expect to pay from $1,000 to $2,000 per day.)

- How will each of the parties be compensated upon completion?

- How will any contingencies be handled?

Once you have an 'in principle' agreement between the parties, the next step is to take the agreement to both your solicitor (see 'Meet Your Team') and accountant to review it and provide advice. Remember, all parties should have signed the agreement before any work commences.

How do you verify the joint venture partner's capabilities?

For most homeowners, their home is their biggest asset. For that reason, you can't afford to take the process of developing your land lightly. On the contrary, it is very important to find the right JV partner to help you with your development. The best way of checking a potential JV partner's capabilities is to check their track record – ask for referrals and call them. Then check the team that will be involved in the process. In addition to the JV partner or property developer (who is essentially the orchestrator of the project), the key people to check are the builder, the architect, the accountant and the solicitor. You can do this by asking the developer or JV partner to provide a list of professionals they use to complete their projects. Check them out online, read their profiles and testimonials, check their past accomplishments and projects, and, if possible, visit completed projects in person, and call them to ask questions. And most importantly, trust your gut. Most of the time, it is right.

Step 4 Checklist

By the end of Step 4, you should have done the following:

- **Visited a lender or mortgage broker to arrange finance for the project, or formed a joint venture partnership.**

- **If applying for a loan, structured the loan accordingly, taking into account the different loan types, timeframes and interest rates.**

- **If entering into a JV partnership, hired a developer and drawn up a contract, with approval from your solicitor and accountant.**

'It is literally true that you can succeed
best and quickest by helping others to succeed.'
– Napoleon Hill

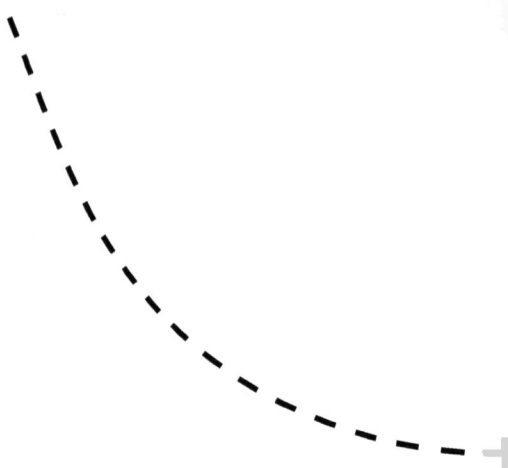

STEP 5: APPLYING FOR YOUR PERMITS
- - - - - - - - - - - - ✕

There are several permits needed for your development before it can be completed. The following figure shows the permits, what is usually required by the council, and for what the permit is used. More in-depth discussion of the various permits follows.

Type	Supporting Documentation	Used For
Planning Permit	Application Form Planning Drawings	Permission to develop a block of land.
Building Permit	Application Form Detailed Drawings Specifications	Permission to build a specific structure using specified materials and methods.

Planning permit

A planning permit is a legal document that gives permission for the use or development of a particular piece of land. To obtain a permit, you must make an application to the local council.

If the council agrees with your proposal, it may grant a planning permit or a 'notice of decision', depending on whether there are any objections to the application. It is a legal notice that states that the council supports the application if the land use or development meets certain conditions. (These conditions are explained on the notice.)

It is important not to confuse planning permits with building permits. Building permits relate to the method of construction of a building or development. If you have a planning permit, you may still need to get a building permit. (Don't worry – we'll discuss this in Step 5.)

So, how do you go about getting a planning permit? In this chapter, I'll walk you through the planning permit process, and give you tips to help speed up the approval process.

Subdivision permit

In all likelihood, your home is sitting on a single lot and therefore that lot is registered under a single title. Subdivision is the process by which your existing title is separated into two or more titles. This is done to make the subsequent sale of any units built both easier and more acceptable to both buyers and home finance organisations (banks for most people).

The process of submitting a subdivision application to council is quite simple. It requires that your architect and land surveyor work together, consulting with the council on those things that impact the final size and location of the resulting lots. The foot print of the units to be built, orientation on the existing block of land, parking, cross-overs (where a driveway crosses a sidewalk) and council minimum lot sizes will all influence the final result.

You have options on when to submit your subdivision application. It can be done simultaneous with your development approval or planning permit or you can wait until construction is complete. We have seen cases where the owner has elected to hold all units constructed as rentals and not submitted a request for subdivision. The fees charged by councils for subdivision can be significant which may influence when you apply.

You might want to submit the permit applications separately from subdivision application. It will avoid any complications that may arise due to changes in unit layouts and drawings that could occur.

Because the subdivision permit is issued contingent on you building what is in your plans, prior to final approval of a subdivision request confirmation that the units were built according to those plans will be required. Therefore a site survey will be conducted to insure a match between the plans submitted and the final product built.

Assuming that there were no unapproved changes to your plans during construction which would result in infringement actions, council will issue your subdivision permit. With those permits in hand you can apply to register the new titles with the appropriate title office.

The planning permit process

There are nine key steps in the planning permit process followed by the majority of councils across Australia. They are:

1. Planning
2. Preparation
3. Submission
4. Council assessment and referrals
5. Public notification

6. Community consultation meeting (if deemed necessary)
7. Assessment by council
8. Reporting and approval
9. Review by civil and administrative tribunal

Here's an overview of each step, with estimated timeframes to give you an idea of how much time it would take to accomplish them.

STEP 1: PLANNING (ONE TO TWO WEEKS)

Find out which zoning applies to your property and meet with a council planner to discuss your project to ensure the best outcome for your permit application. It is advisable to communicate with your neighbours and let them know your plans (more on this in the next section). It is better to do this ahead of time rather than in the middle of the process, to save time and money.

STEP 2: PREPARATION (FOUR TO SIX WEEKS)

Prepare and submit the application form, and pay the fee. You can fill out this form yourself using the checklist that the council provides, or seek guidance from a town planner or architect to ensure quick and efficient processing.

The requirements depend on what type of permit you are applying for but, generally speaking, you will need:

- Planning permit application form.
- Estimated construction and development costs.
- A brief description of the construction works that you need a permit for.

- Certificate of title.
- Copies of your architectural plans and any other documentation the council may need (be sure to check this before you submit your application).

STEP 3: SUBMISSION (ONE WEEK)

Submit the application form and pay the lodgement fee. You may be able to find a list of fees on your local council website. Otherwise, call up and ask.

Pay attention to the application reference number, as this is what you and the council will use in reference to your submission.

STEP 4: COUNCIL ASSESSMENT AND REFERRALS (FOUR TO EIGHT WEEKS)

The planning officer will check your application and then may contact you for additional information. This may take some time, as the council may also solicit feedback from its internal departments (such as engineering, water, service roads, and so on).

STEP 5: PUBLIC NOTIFICATION (FOUR TO SIX WEEKS)

The council may give out public notification if they think your project may have a negative impact on the public, for example if you have a school as a neighbour and your development may limit public car spaces, or you next door neighbour might be affected if you build a second floor therefore overlooking their backyard. The public notification usually comes in the form of direct mail, onsite signage (which you may be responsible for erecting on your own site), or a newspaper advertisement. This will be carried out for fourteen days, during which time anyone in your community, including your neighbours, may submit an objection or support letter regarding the permit you are applying for.

Keep in mind that a public notification may not be necessary if the council has decided that your project will not negatively affect your community.

STEP 6: COMMUNITY CONSULTATION MEETING (THREE TO FOUR WEEKS' ADVANCE NOTICE)

After a period of fourteen days, the council's planning officer will assess your application and then hold a community consultation meeting if necessary. Community consultation meetings are held when there is significant impact on a community, and the council wants to ensure that community input is heard prior to making a decision. This will give the objectors, if any, and the applicant the chance to settle any issues concerning the project.

Disputes between objectors and the applicant can be resolved at this meeting, though this is not often the case. The council may also prepare a report based on your proposal, policies involved, objections received and recommendations.

STEP 7: ASSESSMENT BY COUNCIL (TWO WEEKS)

Some councils have special committees to make decisions on applications for planning permits. At Yarra City Council in Melbourne, for example, this is the Internal Development Approvals Committee (IDAC).

IDAC reviews planning permit applications that have received more than a specific number of objections. That number will be determined by your local council, but normally it's more than five.

STEP 8: REPORTING AND APPROVAL (TWO TO FOUR WEEKS)

Based on the assessment and the community consultation feedback, the council may issue a planning permit immediately, whether there are objections or not. If they approve it despite objections, they will issue a 'Notice of Decision to Grant a Permit' and give out a copy of this notice to objectors as well. The objectors will then be allowed to lodge an application for review at your local civil and administrative tribunal, or CAT (in Victoria, this is VCAT), within twenty-one days. If no objections are filed at CAT, the planning permit will be issued to the applicant.

The council may also decline to grant a permit, even without objectors. A notice of 'Refusal to Grant a Permit' will be issued, explaining why the permit was declined. The applicant will then be given sixty days to apply for review at CAT.

STEP 9: REVIEW BY CIVIL AND ADMINISTRATIVE TRIBUNAL (TWELVE TO FIFTY-TWO WEEKS)

As stated in the previous step, each state has a civil and administrative tribunal, which hears appeals in over 200 areas of civil and administrative matters, residential tenancies, and human rights. The tribunal itself is not a court, as it is a creature of statute and has no inherent jurisdiction or powers. It provides state residents with a low-cost, accessible and independent dispute resolution service, which is deliberately informal and encourages self-representation. Its orders are enforceable by law once they have been registered with the Magistrates' Court.

The civil division hears complaints related to domestic building works, including actions against council decisions or failure of councils to make a decision within a specified time period. The timeframe is determined by the number of complaints filed and capacity of the tribunal to process. Once heard, a complaint is usually acted upon within a few days.

While most councils seek to process all applications as efficiently as possible, there are strict guidelines that must be applied when assessing an application. As such, applicants should have a good understanding of the process, the potential time that it can take to reach a decision, and what influences those time lines.

Realistically, depending on the council, and the size and detail of the proposed works, it can take anywhere from four weeks for small applications, to many months for large-scale development planning permit applications. The more stages one needs to pass through in the assessment process, the longer a decision is likely to take.

TIPS FOR A SPEEDY PERMIT APPROVAL

A speedy permit approval can save you hundreds of thousands of dollars. As an example, for a planning permit application for a 600 square metre expansion in the Melbourne suburb of Clayton, a combination of end-of-calendar-year holidays and a single complaint by a neighbour resulted in cost increases of forty per cent on a recent project. Material cost increases, labour cost increases, and additional town planner and architect costs all combined to increase the overall expenditure and reduce the return on investment. When considering time to market, a residential unit has impacts like any other product.

So, how can you ensure your application is processed as quickly as possible? By following my top tips, outlined here.

Tip 1: Speak to your neighbours in advance

As I discussed in Step 2, it's essential to speak to your neighbours about your proposal, and work openly with council and objectors (if any) to come to a compromise agreement if necessary.

The CAT process is straightforward and reasonably fast once you get a hearing. Getting a hearing, however, can take from twelve to fifty-two weeks, depending on which CAT you are applying to and its current case load. As the CAT encourages self-representation, your legal fees should not be significant, but the impact on your completion time can be. For that reason, it should always be seen as a last resort.

In the interest of saving yourself money, and not delaying your development for months on end, try to resolve any issues you have with your neighbours through communication and negotiation.

Begin communicating with people who have objections as soon as you can, so the problem does not have time to escalate. Make a time for all parties to meet, so any concerns can be heard. When discussing their concerns, stick to the facts and avoid getting emotional.

Remember, when someone makes an objection, it is often due to them feeling they are being ignored. Ensure you hear them out and then confirm with them that you have a complete list of their concerns. Once you have a list of objections, ask them what their ideal solution would be. It may be that you can reach an agreement immediately.

If this is not the case, the next step is to explore solutions to each objection with the other party. Remember, you are looking to find a win-win situation, where everyone is happy with the suggested solution. As part of finding solutions, understand that you will probably need to make some compromises to your plans. To help you do this, keep in mind the bigger picture. At the end of the day, if it means you have to agree to remove a balcony from one of the upstairs bedrooms, it is a small price to pay to resolve any objections immediately and be able to proceed with the project.

Also keep in mind that if you are planning to sell the development at some stage, you want to have your neighbours on your side to make the process of selling go as smoothly as possible.

If you are able to agree on a solution, pass your notes to your legal person to put everything in writing, and have all the parties concerned sign the document.

If you find you are having problems reaching an agreement, you also have the option to bring in a mediator to help bring about a solution that all parties can agree to. Each state has numerous private mediators, as well as public assistance in mediation. These are readily identifiable by performing online searches for property mediation or by calling your local council for a referral to a local mediator.

Lastly, before going to CAT, speak openly with the council – they may tell you that they will issue a permit in spite of a particular objection. An example is objections that a new residence will put a strain on existing school or fire brigade resources.

Tip 2: Speak to a council planner before lodging your planning permit application

If you are concerned about the time it will take to process your application, the council should be able to provide you with an estimated timeframe. Go to their website – all the information is there. You can also make use of any factsheets, guidelines and checklists, which are typically provided by the council with the aim of ensuring that applications are submitted with all the information needed to deliver a speedy response.

As part of learning more about the application process, you should also spend some time reviewing planning permit applications that have previously been submitted to your council. These are usually found on the council's online register. Alternatively, applications can be viewed in person during business hours at the council's offices.

Tip 3: Include all necessary information

Ensure all the necessary information is included in your application when it is lodged. Refer to your over-the-counter meeting notes with council, together with your pre-application meeting notes. Do not hesitate to use the council's checklist, which details all materials that should be included with your application submission. As time is really of the essence here, determine who will prepare each of the components of the application, and confirm the timeline for completing each piece, and then get the professionals working on their various pieces. This will give you the overall lead time necessary to create the application, as well as help you to estimate carrying costs if you are already paying for property financing. Confirm with your town planner or architect who will be putting the application together, who will be reviewing the application before submission, and who will be doing the actual submission.

When making an application, ensure you cover all aspects of the project that will need a planning permit. This saves you the trouble of having to apply for another permit at a later stage. Check with the council planner when lodging the application that all permits you will need are being applied for. Remember, if the appropriate information is not provided in your application, it won't be processed.

Most councils provide a list of their requirements for applications, along with checklists for plans, on their website. You should also check if the council has any local planning policies in their planning scheme that may require specific information to be submitted as part of the application. For example, some councils require developers to specify how they will contribute to or impact local infrastructure such as schools, roads, fire brigades, and so on. Others want to see how your project will contribute to the community's aesthetic or sustainable vegetation.

You should also check if the cost of having the plans stamped is included in the price of the service provided by the architect or building designer to get the planning permit (usually it is not). Plans for a planning permit are stamped separately by:

- The architect, certifying that they meet the Building Code of Australia standards.

- Local water and sewerage agencies, certifying that water and sewerage connections are available.

- The local electrical/gas distribution company, certifying that an electrical connection is available.

- The local telecommunications company, certifying that a telecommunications connection is available.

- The local council (when the application is approved without conditions or upon resubmittal of plans addressing the conditions imposed).

After the planning permit is approved, it may come with conditions that need to be addressed before the plans can be stamped by the council. These conditions can address objections received by the council during the public commentary period, such as installing opaque glass in windows overlooking a neighbour's yard, or protecting a tree from damage during demolition and construction.

It normally takes four to six weeks to alter the plans to account for the conditions, resubmit the application, and then have council act on the updated plans. The town planner or architect will need to address these conditions before the plans are stamped.

The building permit process

The process of applying for a building permit requires the submission of clear and precise working drawings for the proposal. The building permit itself is, in the case of Victoria, submitted via a public or private building surveyor, whom you must select. Working drawings are created during the detail design phase and consist of various views (front, side, back and top) and details of the project (what materials are used where, special considerations to conditions previously identified by the council in their building planning permit approval, and so on), and must be complete and neatly set out with notes and descriptions that are clearly legible. Any builder should be able to read and completely build the property from those plans.

The purpose of working drawings is to allow council the chance to give feedback on the project at an early stage of the process, so any changes required by them can be incorporated by the designer before the full drawings are done and submitted to council for approval. These drawings can also be used by builders to give quotes for the cost of the project.

Working drawings and documentation necessary for a building permit should be prepared by a registered building practitioner, such as a draftsperson.

Different drawings are used for each aspect of the project to give a detailed picture of what the finished product will look like. Drawings commonly required by council when considering a building application include:

- **Site plan**: Also known as a set-out plan, this provides a two-dimensional view of the proposed building/development in relation to the site boundaries. It demonstrates where buildings are to be located on the site.

- **Floor plans**: Floor plans show a two-dimensional view of the proposed building/development layout, showing the individual rooms, their inclusions, and the number of floors.

- **Roof plan**: This is a two-dimensional plan of the whole roof from the perspective of above the building.

- **Elevations**: Elevations are detailed two-dimensional views of every side of the building, as if looking at the building from the outside. They include door and window locations, and the overall building height.

- **Sections**: Sections are two-dimensional cross-sections of different parts of the building to demonstrate the method and materials to be used for construction of each component of the project. This usually includes the subfloor, walls, floor, ceilings and roof.

- **Shadow diagrams**: These are two-dimensional plans that indicate if there are any shadows that may be cast by the building, once constructed, on any neighbouring properties.

- **Landscape plan**: This is a two-dimensional plan showing where plants and trees are to be located on the site, and the species of each. It also indicates lawns, garden beds, and any paved areas such as paths or driveways.

Because of their knowledge of local building codes and regulations, a draftsperson will also be able to request particular permissions to be granted for variations from standard development requirements, such as preferred heights for buildings, minimum setbacks or site layouts. Planning schemes are those ordinances and accompanying maps that detail special (as opposed to standard) development rules/overlays for certain zones, which must be either complied with in your detailed drawings or from which exceptions must be requested. Request for exceptions can be made to vary or remove restrictive covenants, such as exterior building appearance like colour, columns, brick or stone facing. Similarly, requests to set aside or vary easements and rights of way can be made by your design team. Rights of way give another party the right to access parts of your land. These are usually either utility agencies, which have electric, gas or water lines crossing your land, or a neighbour's driveway, which provides access to an otherwise land-locked parcel behind yours.

Other factors the application needs to take into account include conditions relevant to native vegetation offset requirements. These are conditions which councils place on homeowners to encourage the use of native bushes, trees and grasses as opposed to imported or exotic species.

The information and type of plans needed by each council can vary, so begin by contacting the council's planning department to find out exactly what they require to be submitted with a building permit application, and what level of detail is to be included in the plans for the application to be accepted. By educating yourself regarding the council requirements, you will be better positioned to work with the professionals you hire to develop the documentation and drawings for those submissions.

If the plans do not comply with the national building regulations, local laws, or any conditions imposed by the council, amendments will need to be made to the drawings before building approval is granted.

After the building permit is approved, and development and finance conditions have been met, the appointed contractor will commence work.

Step 5 Checklist

By the end of Step 5, you should have done the following:

- **Been to the council with your architect or building designer for a pre-application review of the drawings.**
- **Talked to your neighbours, and taken appropriate measures to settle any potential disputes for the planning permit.**
- **Prepared and submitted your application for planning permit.**
- **Learned how and when to submit your application for a building permit.**

'Patience is not the ability to wait but the ability to keep a good attitude while waiting.'

– Joyce Meyer

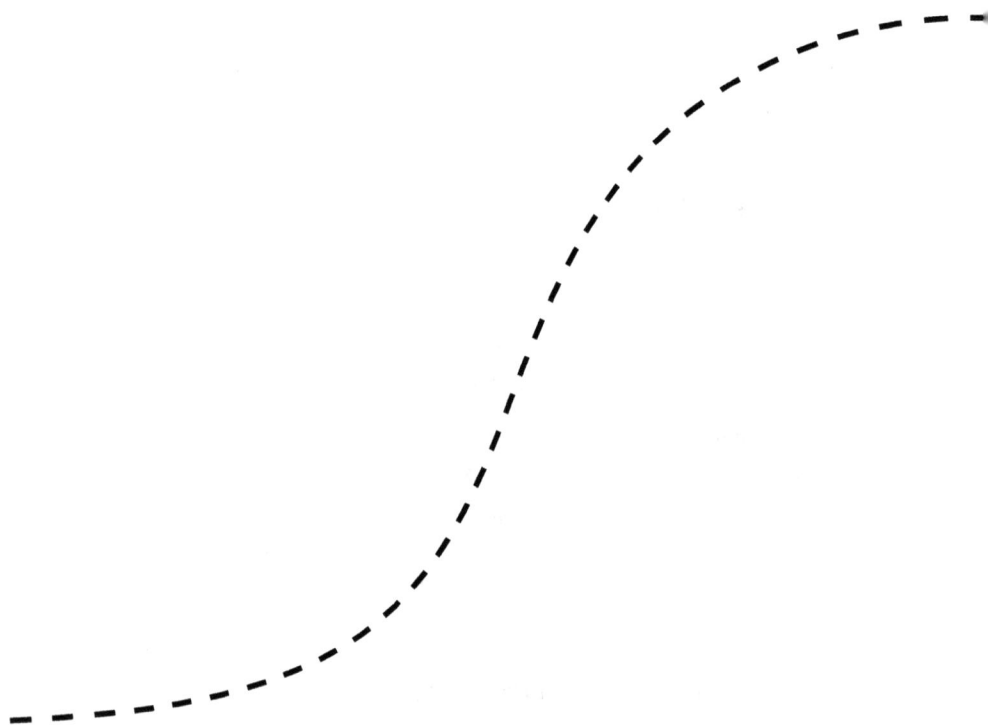

STEP 6: WORKING WITH YOUR BUILDER

Ask people who have undertaken a development project and you will hear stories of great or terrible builders. Thankfully, there are plenty of builders who will work closely with you to confirm the quality level, material selection and form and function of the residential unit you are entrusting them to build.

Given that the quality of your project and the cost of completing that project are ultimately in the hands of your builder, this is arguably the most important step in the process. When it comes to working with a builder, it's imperative that you choose wisely.

A great builder will help you by:

- Identifying opportunities to more efficiently build your project.

- Anticipate issues and recommend solutions.

- Leverage their experience to help you create a contract which requires the fewest possible modifications during construction.

- Resolve day-to-day onsite issues, consulting with you only on those which represent significant quality or cost impacts – without pulling out the contract or raising a variation every time.

This step will lay out for you how to find and work with your builder, how to go about tendering for quotes and drawing up a contract, and take you through the construction process through site supervision and the build.

THE TENDERING PROCESS

By the time you reach this step various consultants have been engaged to help you with the development process. The architect or designer, building surveyor, engineers and quantity surveyor (see 'Building Surveyor', 'Engineers' and 'Quantity Surveyor' in the section 'Meet Your Team') have worked with you to develop the necessary documentation to obtain planning and building permit approval. This included the initial architectural drawings that were used to support the planning permit applications and full detailed drawings and specifications that were used in the application for the building permit. Those detailed drawings and specifications are given to each builder from whom you want a quote. Allow approximately three weeks for a builder to run their numbers, submit clarifying questions, and finally submit their price for the construction of the building. Those clarifying questions are critical as they not only establish clear intent on how and what gets built, but they also allow the builder to put forward variations in both the building approach and materials to be used which could save you time and money in your development. When you tender, please note to all builders that responses to requests for clarifications will be shared with all recipients. In this way, all builders will have the same information and respond with the same level of understanding, thereby permitting you to compare their tenders on an equal basis.

NEGOTIATED TENDER

This is where the preferred builder is chosen first without going through the tendering process. You will not need to build a shortlist of potential builders. You still must negotiate the best price and conditions to complete the work with the preferred builder. This approach is often used where there is a history of the developer or architect and builder working together. It's also very common in residential construction with highly successful outcomes.

I've found the very best outcomes are obtained by builders who actively contribute to the management and execution of the construction project and participate in the crafting of the building contract. Those that can come to the table to discuss ways to make the project better by careful attention to materials, construction techniques, staging of work crews, order of construction, sourcing of materials and finishing touches (paint, flooring, cabinetry, kitchen and bathroom fixtures). Given the high demand for builders, when you find one willing to do some or all of these things, hold on to them!

The tenders will then be reviewed by the architect and/or developer (who may ask those quoting to provide more information), and the architect will then advise you of their recommendation. Be aware that they may not go with the lowest quote. Other factors they will take into account include the builder's capacity to finish the work by the due date, their financial position (if a builder doesn't have enough money to pay their staff, this could delay or even halt your project), and the availability of their supporting staff (engineers, surveyors, and so on).

While your architect or developer will most likely refer a builder, there are times when the homeowner will interview potential builders. As part of the interview process, keep in mind that you need a builder who you can easily talk to you about any aspects of the build that you do not understand or are not happy with. Remember, construction of a house can take several months (or even longer if you are waiting for approval from council on some aspects of the build), so you need to be sure that you have easy and open communication with them. Take the time to meet the builder and discuss your project. The cost of a tea or a lunch is small in comparison to the insight you will gain.

You should also agree with the builder about how often you will receive updates from them on the progression of the project (and they should come to you immediately if they have any issues that need to be resolved). It is important that you stick to what you have both agreed to, so that you don't interfere with them getting on with the job.

You also need to ensure the builder you select has all the necessary insurance to cover the work they do.

Builders insurance

The builder must provide you with a copy of their builders' insurance policy, and a program scheduling the start and completion dates of the construction phase. Any builder you use must be registered and have up-to-date insurance. To verify if they are registered, go to alwayscheckyourbuilder.com.au.

Also, before providing a deposit, a builder needs to provide you with a 'certificate of currency', which is issued by the insurer and states that the policy is current. (According to the Master Builders Association of Victoria, if the final quote for the work is $20,000 or more, the builder is entitled to a five per cent deposit. If the quote is less than $20,000, then a maximum deposit of ten per cent is allowed).

Other states have varying requirements. As builders and insurance are regulated at the state level, each state may have different thresholds and requirements for their builders and the insurance they must carry. Check with your particular state to determine your builder's requirements. The table below provides additional detail on individual state and territory regulations as well as the names of agencies to visit.

ACT	Known as Residential Building Warranty insurance, it covers homeowners for loss of deposit, incomplete or defective building work if their builder dies, disappears or becomes insolvent. It's a requirement for residential building work valued over $12,000.	www.planning.act.gov.au
NSW	The Home Building Compensation Fund covers homeowners for loss of deposit, incomplete and defective building work if their builder dies, disappears, becomes insolvent or fails to satisfy a money order (resulting in the suspension of their licence by NSW Fair Trading). It's a requirement for most residential building work valued over $20,000 (other than the construction of new buildings of more than three storeys, containing two or more dwellings).	www.icare.nsw.gov.au

NT	In the Northern Territory, builders warranty insurance isn't a legal requirement at the time of writing.	nt.gov.au
QLD	Known as Home Warranty insurance, it's provided solely by the Queensland Building and Construction Commission.	www.qbcc. qld.gov.au
SA	Known as Building Indemnity insurance, it covers homeowners for loss of deposit, incomplete or defective building work if their builder dies, disappears or becomes insolvent. It's a requirement for residential building work valued over $12,000.	www.cbs. sa.gov.au
TA	In Tasmania, builders warranty insurance is a voluntary scheme and not a legal requirement.	www. worksafe.tas. gov.au
VIC	Known as Domestic Building Insurance (DBI), it covers homeowners for loss of deposit, incomplete or defective building work if their builder dies, disappears, becomes insolvent or fails to comply with a tribunal or court order. It's a requirement for residential building work valued over $16,000.	www. consumer.vic. gov.au
WA	Known as Home Indemnity insurance, it covers homeowners for loss of deposit, incomplete or defective building work if their builder dies, disappears or becomes insolvent. It's a requirement for residential building work valued over $20,000.	www. commerce. wa.gov.au

The three types of insurance a builder should carry are domestic building/builders warranty insurance, professional indemnity insurance and public liability insurance.

1: DOMESTIC BUILDING/BUILDERS WARRANTY INSURANCE

Some states require a builder to have building insurance. For example, in Victoria, for any work worth more than $16,000, a builder needs to have domestic building insurance, in Australian Capital Territory (ACT) It's called builders warranty, a requirement for residential building work valued over $12,000. This covers the costs of repairs up to $300,000 to fix any structural defects found in the building (such as cracks in the foundation) for a period of six years after completion, and any non-structural defects (such as a leaky roof) found after completion for a period of two years. This protects the homeowner and ensures the work will be completed in the event of the builder not finishing the work.

In cases where work is completed but defects are later found during the warranty period, the builder must fix any defects or pay for the work to be done. The homeowner will have to submit a claim to the builder's insurance company in the event that the work is not completed within the required timeframe (which can differ from state to state). The timeframe in which an insurance company responds is also dependent on the individual company, but maximum time periods are established by each state's insurance commissioner. See the table above for information about your state.

2: PROFESSIONAL INDEMNITY INSURANCE

Your builder needs to have this insurance if, in addition to their work as a builder, they perform any of the following roles during the project *(see 'Meet your Team' for descriptions of each of these roles):*

- Design, including advice in relation to design, in accordance with all relevant building, construction or engineering codes and standards.
- Drafting.
- Technical calculation.
- Technical specifications.
- Construction and project management.
- Building surveying or inspecting.
- Quantity surveying.
- Engineering (geotechnical/soil engineer, structural engineer, civil engineer, acoustic engineer, hydraulic engineer).

The services above must be either performed by or under the direct supervision of one of the following:

1. A properly registered engineer, architect or surveyor.

2. A quantity surveyor who is a member of the Australian Institute of Quantity Surveyors.

3. A licensed professional recognised by the building trade as competent to complete such work.

3: PUBLIC LIABILITY INSURANCE

This covers the builder against legal liability that may result from any claim made by another party during completion of the work. For example, civil suits claiming bodily injury from construction materials left on the roadside or footpath, which cause an accident.

The contract

After the tender is finalised and a builder has been selected, a building contract will be drawn up for the homeowner and contractor to formalise. Your selected builder will have a preferred template that they want to use. You can also find templates of these contracts on the websites of the following bodies:

- The Australian Building Industry Contracts (ABIC)
- The Australian Institute of Architects
- The Master Builders Association in your state or territory
- The Property Council of Australia
- The Housing Institute Association

WHAT IS GOING TO BE BUILT?

The first definitive view of how much the build will cost is when you receive the builder's tender quoting their price. This is a starting point from which, through negotiations both before and during the project, items will be added and deleted, each time resulting in a potential change in price.

The following list represents what you should expect to see in the builder's quote and which should carry forward to the contract you sign with the builder. These are in addition to the detailed specifications from your architect. Whatever form and however long the list in the quote is – read it, understand it, and understand the ramifications of making any changes to that list.

Dates (when it will be built)

    Start date (or events upon which start date is determined)

    Completion date

    Delays allowed for

Payments

    Deposit if any

    Progress – amounts and work to have been completed to qualify
        for such a payment

Site costs

    Occupational health & safety requirements

        Engineering work

    Soil tests

    Excavation

    Driveway (normally extra)

    Landscaping (normally extra)

    Fencing (normally extra)

Specifications

    Appliances

    Lighting

    Window treatment (fly screens, tinting, shades)

    Painting

Allowances & prime cost items

    Make sure that the amounts set aside for these things are
        reasonable

Flooring

    Wood

    Carpet

    Tile/stone

Kitchen/Bathrooms

    Counter tops

    Tapware (faucets)

    Shelving in pantries

Bedrooms

    Built-ins – shelving, drawers, rods in closets

Definitions of key words and phrases

Warranties provided

Insurance provided

Acknowledgements – site is suitable

Plans and specifications – from architect

HOW MUCH WILL IT COST YOU TO BUILD IT? CONTRACTUAL PAYMENT TERMS AND CONDITIONS.

There are various types of payment terms linked to contracts available for a building agreement. They include:

Lump sum or fixed price

This is where the builder and developer/homeowner agree to a price for the whole project (including the cost of materials) in advance. This type of contract breaks down that fixed price into progress payments, which are paid out based on the builder's progress. A variation on this is a fixed price on labour with a not-to-exceed price on materials, or an actual price on materials (no mark-up by the builder).

Cost-plus

This type of contract pays the builder for their stated costs plus a set amount of profit, which is typically an agreed percentage of the total value of the project. This type of contract is not unusual in relation to residential construction, and often useful when the owner or developer is not sure of what they want.

Schedule of rates

A schedule of rates is a list of market values used by the industry for materials or labour, and is used by the builder when tendering for a project. If builders respond with these rates and do not ask clarifying questions, you probably don't want that builder on your job. Either they feel that the job is so simple that they do not need to engage in a discussion beforehand, or they are busy already, so why not throw some big number around to see if you will bite?

ADVICE

Before we move on, a word of caution: Because of the complexity of a building contract, it is highly advisable that you ask both your solicitor and architect to examine it before signing.

A common mistake I see among new developers is signing contracts without getting industry or legal advice. Industry advice will help you to identify those areas of a project most prone to variations – those documents which detail costs for materials, labour, or permits not covered in the contract between you and the builder. By focusing on those 'hotspots' in a contract, you can double-check your decisions on what you want built and how you want it built. This may lead you to revise the contract – and it is better to revise it before final signature and avoid costly variations later.

Some builders use terminology that requires both a general definition of the word, as well as what it means for the construction process. Your industry adviser (project manager, developer, architect or solicitor) can help with some real-life examples of what words like 'extras' imply.

Your legal adviser can help you to understand what happens in the best of cases when everything gets built as originally planned, and there are no surprises during construction. This includes how much you pay, when you pay it, and confirming that the builder is both licensed and insured correctly. That same legal adviser can also advise you on worst-case scenarios, such as what happens if the builder goes bankrupt, or when the builder asks for a progress payment without progress being made or signed off by the local council inspectors, or how disputes regarding the contract are resolved and the potential financial impact on you.

Site supervision

On a project such as this, it is only natural that you will want to get updates from the construction team as to how they are progressing. It is important, though, that you give the builder space to allow them to do their job. Every time you show up on site, the rhythm of work has to change and delays are introduced – so schedule your onsite visits and stick to the schedule. If you feel the pressing need to go and see how things are progressing, wait until the builder's crew has left for the day. Also keep in mind that many builders view the job site as theirs until it is returned to you – so inform your builder if you are stopping by after hours.

Having said that, make sure you have someone monitoring the builder's progress. Unless you have experience in project management, it is important that someone be appointed as construction supervisor/project manager. Obviously, this role should not be filled by the builder or any of the builder's subcontractors. This person is often someone from the architect's office. Their job is to confirm, periodically, that the construction is following the submitted plans, identify issues, and work with the builder to develop solutions to present to you. They are also responsible for resolving any variation requests, or disputes that may arise with the contractor regarding what is in or out of the scope of the contract.

Variations and extras

A common variation request is when material identified in the plans is not available when needed. For example, the builder may advise that the marble tiles they have ordered are out of stock and that the replacement tiles are more expensive. In cases such as this, look for a solution where changes are kept to a minimum, as the builder may use this as an opportunity to charge a higher rate than the price they quoted in the tender.

When my neighbour developed three units on her site, she ended up paying $300,000 more in 'extras and variations' for her construction when she changed her mind about the type of floor covering, countertop materials, light fixtures, closet contents (shelving, hanging rod, drawers), garden finishes (grass, flowers, trees, bushes), and the brand name and models of heating and air conditioning units.

But this also offers an opportunity for you to make any last-minute changes to things like finishings and specifications, if necessary. For example, a manufacturer may have recalled the model of the heating and air conditioning unit that you had specified, and you need to make a change.

When the construction has been completed, the architect or project manager will prepare a list of any incomplete or irregular finishing items, such as flooring, painting, tiling, and so on. This is commonly referred to as a punch list, and the builder will reply back as to how soon the list will be completed. Final payment to the builder is normally contingent on the completion of the list. This is the stage where the project manager will collect from the builder all the warranties and guarantees for fittings like the water heater, air conditioning, and kitchen equipment.

Step 6 Checklist

By the end of Step 6, you should have done the following:

- Amended any details of the design in order to comply with the conditions attached to the council's planning approval.

- Sought tenders for the building of the project and selected a builder.

- Obtained proof of insurance from the builder.

- Receive the official building permit.

- Signed the building contract and set a start date for the project to begin.

- Appointed a building supervisor and a project manager.

- Obtained full working drawings from the architect, and a complete list of materials with specifications.

- Had the architect or building designer compile a list of any incomplete or irregular finishing items once construction is completed.

- Collected warranties and guarantees for all fittings and kitchen equipment from the builder.

'Challenges are what make life interesting
and overcoming them is what makes life meaningful.'
– Joshua J. Marine

STEP 7: GO TO MARKET

✕- - - - - - - - - - - - -

Depending on your exit strategy, you could go to market at a number of different stages. You could sell your house as is, you could sell your house with council-approved plans, you could subdivide and sell individual lots, or you could go to market and sell off–the-plan or with a developed property – either to sell, or to rent.

The stage when you go to market will affect both the costs of your project as well as the likely return. As a general rule, the numbers (both cost and return) will go up the further you progress your development.

Whether you intend to sell your existing home, sell your land, sell your developed property or rent it out, you'll need to first find a real estate agent to help you find buyers or tenants, and then present your land/property in the best possible light so it attracts the best price.

How to find a good real estate agent

For details on the benefits of working with a real estate agent, see 'Meet Your Team'. This discussion, on the other hand, will focus on how to find the right agent to take your property to market.

Start by looking online. While some agents are generalists that deal with all types of sales and rentals, other agents specialise in land only, off-the-plan sales, new construction sales or rental management. Focus on the type of agent who aligns with your exit strategy. Check out realestate.com.au and domain.com.au to see the different properties that have recently been sold in your area. For each of the properties, take note of the names of the agents, along with how many properties they have sold. The agents with the most sales are a good starting point for your shortlist. There are plenty of websites that allow you to find and compare agents, including ratemyagent.com.au, agentselect.com.au, localagentfinder.com.au, and openagent.com.au, to see how they are perceived by the local community, and the quality of their reviews. This could help you further narrow down your shortlist, or prioritise who you'd like to meet with first.

You should then arrange to meet with the agents on your shortlist for an interview, preferably at your property. Questions to have in mind when meeting with them include:

- **What is your fee and what other costs do I need to pay?** The commission will vary from location to location, though it typically ranges from 1 per cent to 2.5 per cent (off-the-plan commission is from two to four per cent). If the property price is higher, the percentage of the commission is lower. For example, if the value of the property is $1 million, the commission is more likely to be 1 per cent to 1.5 per cent of the sale price. If the property is valued at $500,000, it would be between 1.5 per cent and 2.5 per cent, though sometimes more. For this reason, you should aim to speak with at least three different agents – to have an understanding of the commission charged in the area.

- **Would you list the property for sale or for auction, and why?** The best option may be an auction because of the emotional pressure of the competition (multiple bidders), which prompts buyers to pay a higher price. The market activity closer to the date for your sale will influence the decision. If there are many properties similar to yours going to auction in your area and not obtaining the reserve bids, a private sales approach may be considered by the agent.

- **How long do you think it will take to sell the property?** If the price is set right, it normally takes four to six weeks.

- **Do you have references from previous clients who can be contacted?** It is always helpful to get insights from other people who have worked with the agent. Try to get a couple of names and numbers of previous clients, if you can.

You should also pay attention to each agent's level of professionalism and organisation. Here are some additional questions to take into consideration:

- Did they answer the phone when you called to schedule a meeting, or get back to you in less than four hours?

- Were they on time for the meeting, and did they come prepared with a list of comparable properties (both for sale and recently sold) in your area?

- Did they demonstrate their knowledge of the local market, and the relevance of comparable properties in the market?

- Did they outline the marketing campaign they would oversee to sell your property, as well as selling costs and the inspection process?

Based on the answers to these questions, select the agent or agency that best suits your needs.

Before we move on, a few words of caution: There are real estate agents who will allow you to set the sale price above the market, so they can gain the listing. Then, once he or she has the listing, their approach is to reduce your expectation and bring the price back in line with the market. It is best to select an agent who can accurately estimate the price for your home based on market conditions and go with their estimate.

It's also important to compare apples with apples. For example, let's say a property in the same street as yours recently sold for $1.1 million, and the agent is saying that your property is worth only $900,000. The difference might be that the first home has been renovated and extended, and is ready to be occupied, while your home is in need of an upgrade and renovation. Ask to see internal pictures of the properties that the agent is comparing with yours. This will help you ensure the agent is making (relatively) fair comparisons.

Negotiating a deal

Once you've chosen your agent, there are five key aspects you need to cover off before you get started. They are as follows.

1. CONDITIONS OF ENGAGEMENT

The agent will request that you engage them exclusively for a set period (usually ninety days). This means they are the sole agent for the sale of the property. Also, if the property sells during this time, no matter what the circumstances, they are to be paid the specified commission. For instance, if the architect you engaged decides to buy the property, you still owe a commission to the agent, even though the architect was working on the project before the agent was signed on. You can engage an agent on a non-exclusive basis, but the agents will work harder on the exclusive listings.

2. COMMISSION STRUCTURE

The commission you pay to the agent for selling the property can be done as a flat rate or on a sliding scale.

On a flat rate, the agreed percentage (say 2.5 per cent) is applied to the sale price to calculate the commission owing to the agent. For a sliding scale, you agree to pay a lower rate (say two per cent) up to a certain sale price (say $1.2 million). For a sale price above that figure, the agent then gets a higher percentage (say ten per cent).

For example, if the property is estimated to sell for $1.2 million, you can negotiate for the agent to get a commission rate of two per cent up to $1.25 million, and ten per cent of any money paid above that amount.

So, if the property sold for $1.3 million, the agent would get two per cent on the first $1.25 million ($25,000) and ten per cent of the extra $50,000 ($5,000), bringing the total commission payable to $30,000. If you were paying a flat rate of 2.5 per cent to sell the property, you would be paying $32,500 in commission to the agent on a sale price of $1.3 million.

The sliding scale approach can be an effective strategy, as it motivates the agent to get a price above what you were expecting. But when you are negotiating with the agent, make sure the price that triggers a higher percentage is above the quoted market value of the property. You should also make sure the commission percentage rate you are quoted by the agent is inclusive of GST.

3. MARKETING

There's a list of normal expenses when selling your property, all related to marketing. This list includes professional photos, online marketing, signboards, a floor plan and three-dimensional designs, copywriting, newspaper and magazine advertisements, brochures and postcard drop-offs.

Your property advertisement will be competing with thousands of others, so you want it to stand out as much as possible. To achieve this, you need a professional photographer to take photos of the property, as well as a floorplan designer and a copywriter. The real estate agent will organise all of these services for you. The cost will most likely be around $500, depending on the number of photos you want taken, and the time of day they're taken. If you're trying to sell or rent a fully developed property, try to have the photos taken at dusk. They cost slightly more (as they are taken after working hours and take longer), but the effect is amazing.

The marketing costs for promoting the property are paid by you, the owner. These days, almost all buyers in Australia do their search for real estate online. The two main sites are realestate.com.au and domain.com.au, and your agent will typically have a package whereby they will list your property as featured/new listing on both sites for thirty to forty-five days. After that, the advertisement stays online as normal listing until the property is sold. This advertisement typically costs $2,000 to $3,000.

In addition, the agent should oversee the creation of a property brochure and hand out postcard-type flyers (this costs around $300), containing key information about the property, along with pictures and a floor plan. Depending on the area, the agent may also suggest advertising the property in the local newspaper. If the property is to be sold as a house-and-land package or off the plan, it will be necessary to prepare three-dimensional drawings to give prospective buyers a clear vision of what the finished property will look like. The cost for this type of promotion is around $5,000.

Most agents also have their own database of buyers, whom they contact when they have a new property for sale.

An agent will also oversee the creation of a signboard, which will have pictures of the property's interior, information on the number of bedrooms and bathrooms, and any key selling points for the property. A signboard (which typically costs $450 to $1,000) also helps pinpoint the location of the property for buyers who are not familiar with the area.

A typical marketing campaign will cost between $2,500 and $6,500 and it can be charged upfront or upon sale of the property.

4. LISTING APPROACH

When it comes to selling your property, you have two options: Hold an auction, or list the property for sale at a set price (private sale).

Option 1: Auction

The aim of an auction is to have all the interested buyers bidding against each other for the property. An advantage of this approach is that the property often sells for a price above expectation, as potential buyers become determined to outbid each other in order to secure the property.

Let me give you an example, regarding one particular property I was involved at auction. When I started talking to the agent about four weeks before the auction, the indicative selling price was $840,000 to $890,000. I asked the agent if the vendor would accept an offer prior to the auction, and he said no. When I called again two weeks before the auction, he informed me that because of the huge interest, the indicative selling price had jumped up to $890,000 to $930,000, so the vendor was even more determined to wait for the auction. On auction day, our group bought this property for $1.035 million (our mark was $1.1 million). Afterwards, the vendor told me she was shocked how much the property had sold for. Her expectation was a maximum of $900,000.

The challenge with this approach is that if you do not have many (or any) interested buyers to drive demand, the property may not reach the price you were hoping for.

Option 2: Private sale

The advantage of listing the property for a set price is that, based on the comparables, you have a better estimate of how much you will get for the sale, and this can help when you are doing budgets for the project. The first four weeks the property is on the market are the most important. The reason is that your property will show as a new listing on the major real estate sites (realestate.com.au and domain.com.au) and at the top of buyers' search results. The longer your property remains on the market, the further down it will appear in these lists. Even if your property *does* continue to appear, if the price is not right, you will lose valuable prospects.

With that in mind, you need to set the right price from the beginning. If you set the price too high, you might lose momentum, in the sense that buyer interest could dwindle. This means your property will sit on the market longer than you want and can afford.

The challenge of listing the property at a fixed price is that, if you set it too low, it will sell immediately, and you will be left feeling that you may have been able to get more money for it.

Ask the agent their thoughts on the best approach for your property. It is important that your agent can demonstrate to you what they feel is the best option to take.

As part of the sales process, your agent should also call or email you with any feedback offered by potential buyers during property inspections.

This should happen no later than the next business day. If your price expectation isn't set right, you can act quickly to adjust the price and avoid losing momentum.

Property inspections should be held by the agent at least twice a week, preferably with one on the Saturday as this is when most families set aside time to inspect properties. The agent should arrange private inspections for prospective buyers who can't attend on the scheduled dates.

The time a property will be on the market (depending on the area, and assuming it has been priced correctly) is about four to six weeks. Most properties passed in at auction (when bids do not meet the minimum price set by the owner) will typically sell within a few days, as your agent will continue negotiations with other potential buyers who inspected the property and attended the auction. Generally speaking, the vendor is more determined to let the property go in this instance, as they have already stress-tested the market for the best possible price for their property.

5. Expenses

The agent should detail any other expenses you are liable for outside their commission and marketing costs. For example, if a courier is used to send a contract to you or the purchaser, who pays the fee? Make sure you get everything in writing so there is no confusion at a later stage.

Renting your property

If you decide to rent rather than sell your property, this comes with its own set of benefits and challenges. Keeping the property as a rental is a great way to increase your income or pension. Also, while the rent is taxable, it can be offset by the expenses attributable to the rental and interest repayments on your loan. The other benefit is that in the history of Australia, a property will generally double in value over seven to ten years. So, the longer you hold on to it, the more it will rise in value.

There are several ways you can find a tenant for your property. Firstly, you can place an advertisement in the local paper or online. In both cases, it can often be free of charge. If you decide to advertise online, there are several companies that offer this service. One of them is rent. com.au, which allows you to advertise your property for free. It also allows you to screen potential tenants, at a cost of about $25.

Once you've found a tenant, you can manage the property yourself or let a property management company do it for you.

Secondly, most real estate agencies will have a rental department. Their fees are reasonably cheap given the amount of work involved in managing a rental property, so if you're looking for a hassle-free option, this is the way to go. They will advertise your property, find and screen the tenant (you can view the tenant's application and the decision to let the property to them is yours), collect the rent on your behalf, and inspect the property every six months, taking pictures of the condition of the house and informing you of the results of the inspection. The tenant will pay a one-month bond, which can be accessed if the tenant doesn't pay rent or damages the property in some way.

Property management fees range from five per cent to seven per cent of the weekly rental amount, plus one to two weeks' rent for the letting fee. This fee (which is charged in addition to the monthly administration fee), is the amount charged for finding a tenant. For example, if you are renting your property for $500 per week, you will pay $1,000 (two weeks' rent) for the letting fee, plus $35 per week (seven per cent of the weekly rent).

The market is always competing for more business, so property management companies are often willing to negotiate the letting fee and the commission. Also, you are typically required to pay a marketing fee to advertise the property for rent. Depending on the company, this can be between $100 and $300, charged every time your property becomes vacant.

The finishing touches

If you want to maximise the sale or rental potential of your home, there's one more thing you should consider: Home staging. This is where a vacant home is either fully or partially furnished prior to inspection.

The goal is to make the home appealing to the highest number of potential buyers or tenants, thereby selling or leasing the property more swiftly, and often for more money.

Home staging in Australia has been rising in popularity over the past ten years. This is because a house with furniture typically sells faster and for a higher price than one that is empty.

Furniture helps prospective buyers more easily imagine that this could be their home. According to the real estate agents, staging a home makes it easier for a buyer to visualise the property as their future home.

There are companies that specialise in staging houses for sale and for rent. The best way to find one is to talk to your real estate agent – they will know the best options available, and they will be happy to organise this for you.

The best time to stage your house for sale is from the date you put your house on the market. After all, you want all that beautiful furniture to be there before you have professional photos taken to showcase your house. This will also make your agent's job a lot easier during property inspections, as they won't have to help potential buyers imagine how wonderful it would be to live there. So why not spend $5,000 or so to stage your house (this price is based on a small, three-bedroom house), when you could get an extra $25,000 for it?

Step 7 Checklist

By the end of step 7, you should have done the following:

- Negotiated terms with a real estate agent to either sell the property for you or find tenants for it.

- Made a decision as to whether you want to stage the home and, if so, hired a home staging company to undertake this task.

> *'It's time to move on, time to get going.*
> *What lies ahead, I have no way of knowing.*
> *But under my feet, baby, grass is growing.'*
> **– Tom Petty**

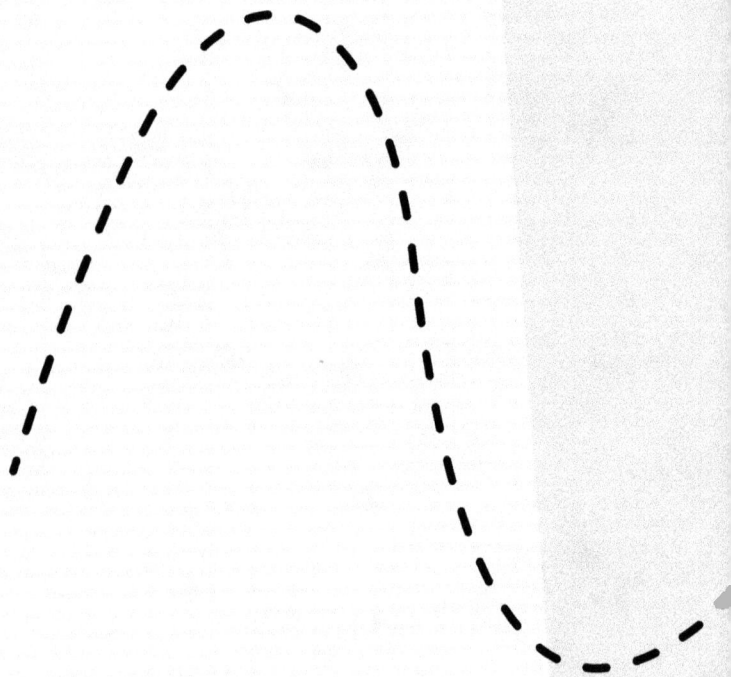

MEET
YOUR TEAM

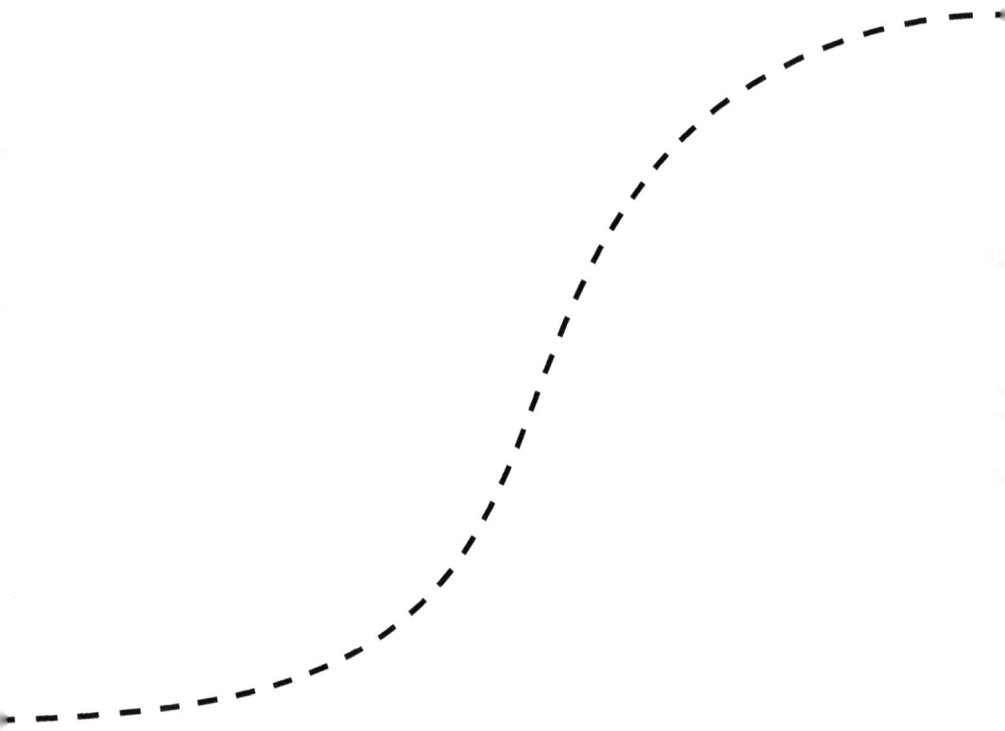

MEET YOUR TEAM

One of the biggest mistakes I see new developers making is trying to develop or subdivide without the help of professionals. This is a situation where trying to save money can really come back to haunt you.

The money you pay to professionals for their legwork and advice is an investment that will pay for itself many times over in saved time and expenditure. It will also give you peace of mind, knowing that everything has been done professionally, and in accordance with council and government requirements.

Throughout Section 1, I indicated the stages at which you should hire or engage certain professionals. In this section, I'll provide an overview of each of those professionals, plus a few others you may need along the way. I've presented these professionals in the order you'll need them, but you will find that you need to engage multiple professionals at once. You'll also notice that some of the descriptions for professionals are longer than others, depending on the importance of each professional in the success of the project.

THE IMPORTANCE OF HIRING THE RIGHT PROFESSIONALS

Julian and his family decided to develop the backyard of their family home in the Melbourne suburb of Ashburton, with the plan to use the profits as a deposit for a bigger home.

They wanted to build something contemporary, which would be in line with what the council would allow them to build. They chose modern colours and textures so the re-saleability of the property was maximised.

However, while nothing big went wrong, it wasn't smooth sailing – one of Julian's neighbours objected to the plans, the council kept knocking them back with little advice about changes they should make, and it took longer than expected.

One of the bigger hiccups was the technical engineering firm Julian initially engaged.

'It was clear, even to a layperson, that their set of drawings for my drainage plan wouldn't work. They actually had water flowing upwards at one point. So, I had to engage a different firm to get the plans redesigned. Later, when the builder engaged the designer about the mistake, the designer wouldn't accept responsibility because he knew he could be financially liable for the error.'

He also hired a draftsperson to do the drawings and a surveyor to help him get through the process.

One of the lessons he took from the experience was that he'd prefer to work with individuals rather than big companies next time, as he would be able to have more one-on-one interaction with them. He could remember making many phone calls and doing a lot of running around, trying to get hold of people in the bigger organisations.

'You need to be very careful about who you engage and why you engaged them. I didn't necessarily go out and engage professionals on price but I think that you need to engage a professional who is going to be part of that journey with you and understands how to work with you.'

The accountant

Ideally, you should obtain the services of an accountant who is experienced in the field of real estate development. Not only can such a resource save you thousands in taxes with the correct advice, but they can also help to set up the accounts, policies and procedures you will need to use from the outset of your project.

An accountant fully understands the tax implications of subdividing your property. This is of particular importance when it comes to such issues as capital gains tax (CGT) when you come to sell the development, and whether you will be liable for goods and services tax (GST). They also advise on how you should account for fees paid to professionals or the council, as well as interest incurred on loans during construction.

First, ensure the accountant is open to frequent calls from you as you commence with the development, until such time as the system becomes familiar to you. This is particularly important if the concept of developing is entirely new to you. Find an accountant who is happy to answer all of your questions until you become more educated about the process of developing.

The accountant will also be able to advise on how you can best structure the development for tax purposes. Your options could include undertaking the project as an individual, a single proprietor, a limited liability partnership, a trust or a joint venture.

The next step is understanding the system recommended by the accountant to record expenses and report them. From that point forward, your relationship should be one of reviewing monthly reports and submitting to your accountant whatever questions might arise, especially the ones related to taxes you need to pay (like CGT, GST, margin scheme, income tax, and so on).

The solicitor or lawyer

When it comes to the legal side of things and preparing for a subdivision and/or property development, your approach should be that it is better to pay a little upfront for a qualified solicitor than risk losing your profits – or possibly everything – later. Look for and hire a solicitor who specialises in property.

When it comes to property subdivision and development, there is no such thing as a standard contract. Builders, developers and most professionals you deal with will have their own version of a contract that they will ask you to sign. In each case, it is worth paying to have a solicitor look the contract over so you understand exactly what it is that you are agreeing to when you sign it.

The combination of a good accountant and a good solicitor forms a solid legal and financial foundation for both you and your builder or developer.

There are a host of issues the solicitor will provide advice on, and then act on your behalf. They typically include (but are not limited to):

- Creating a legal structure for the development project.

- Providing interpretation on council rulings.

- Advice on seeking exceptions to existing rules and regulations.

- Contract (sales, developments, and so on).

- Contract development and/or review of third-party contracts offered by developers, builders, real estate agents, tradespeople, and so on.

While referrals are important, unless they are based on very recent interactions, the reliability of the information changes with time. Bear in mind, too, that solicitors also change support staff. So, consider the following questions when reviewing a solicitor to act on your behalf:

- Does the solicitor spend the majority of their time practising real estate law with an emphasis on development?

- Do they have a minimum of five years of practice?

- Do they currently represent builders and developers?

- Is there any potential for conflict of interest? For instance, do they represent any builder or developer who you are considering using?

Before your first meeting with a solicitor, ask them for information on the following:

- **How do they charge for this type of work?** (Always try to set a fixed price, as you can't control the time it takes to complete each task.)

- **Do they charge for the initial consultation?** (Normally, you have a thirty-minute free consultation to talk about your needs, but always ask upfront if they charge for this.)

- **Is there a retainer you need to pay upfront that they draw down from, or do they bill periodically?** (Sometimes they will charge a retainer – whereby you pay an amount upfront to cover future expenses – and will withdraw from it as needed.)

- **What is the mix of experience levels within the solicitor's office?** (Some solicitors have junior staff who they charge out at rates much lower than those of a senior partner. Ask for the fee schedule.)

The town planner

Reminder to the reader: Councils engage town planners as permanent staff members and, in smaller councils, under contract for ad-hoc work. What you the reader need to focus on is how a town planner can be hired by you to make your permitting process easier.

Although a town planner works alongside with the architect they can apply for a planning permit on your behalf, and provide you with feedback on your development application and its chance of approval by the council. They can also provide information on aspects of the development which do not comply with local and state government laws, and help to ensure the application has all the elements it needs before formal submission to the council. In essence, they save you time.

Should the council decide it needs more information from you before it can make a decision about your application, the town planner can be contacted by your architect or building designer for guidance on how best to redraft any submitted plans in response to the council's request.

You can request a meeting with your town planner, and they will answer questions and provide advice. You should take all the necessary materials (title of the property, drawings, photographs, proposal, and past plans if you have them) to the meeting, and have your architect or building designer go with you.

The real estate agent

A good real estate agent has a wealth of local information on what styles of property are in demand, what amenities are popular among certain buyers (restaurants, cafés, shops, parks, and so on), and whether to finish your development to a medium, high, or luxurious standard and can therefore save you thousands of dollars by advising you upfront on what to build (not how).

It is critical that you obtain advice from the best local real estate agent you can find for your neighbourhood. You are after local knowledge of the area, recent sales and listing information, as well as someone who will remember your development should they have an off-the-plan buyer looking in your neighbourhood (if you're selling off the plan).

There are three main benefits that a real estate agent brings to the team.

1. Advice on what will sell in a particular neighbourhood. This includes the number of bedrooms and bathrooms, garage or no garage, and so on. Everything down to details of the type of floor covering, colour of paint to be used, lighting, and outdoor garden ideas. This advice needs to be sought out early so it can be incorporated into the initial design plans (prior to submittal for the request for a planning permit and the later request for a building permit).

2. Price guidance. The agent will be able to provide an accurate price range for both the existing house and also what the new development would sell for if it was on the market today, and what the off-the-plan price point would be. The agent will also have information on which banks or mortgage providers are active in the area.

3. They can list and sell the property as it is, with plans approved, as subdivided lots, off-the-plan, or post-construction.

4. Re-read the first two sections in Step 7 ('How to find a good real estate agent' and 'Negotiating a deal').

The property valuer

Property valuers are normally engaged by banks, financial institutions, developers and buyers to provide independent valuation on properties. In your case, a property valuer would be retained by you to confirm the opinion of a local real estate agent.

So, the question is: Should you invest in a property valuer (the cost of a value report typically ranges from $800 to $1,500) when the local real estate agent has already provided you with a free estimate on the value of your current property and on the probable sales point for the yet-to-be-built development? I believe you should.

There's one major reason why you should also have a price estimate (valuation) done by a property valuer: Independence. In most of Australia, a formal valuation is a complex process and can only be provided by a property valuer who has undertaken the necessary training, as the report will be carefully prepared to contain all the relevant factors of a particular property. A valuer makes a very detailed comparison of the market, taking into consideration the land value and the building value. The valuation is not tainted by ulterior motives, such as the potential for commission, and will therefore be seriously considered by banks, developers and potential buyers.

In contrast, a real estate agent only gives his or her opinion based on their local experience, and any estimated value of the property is obtained by comparing it to other similar properties recently sold. Also, an agent will sometimes give a higher figure in the hope of earning the listing, whereas a valuer has no incentive to make up the value.

Your best place to start when seeking out a property valuer is the Australian Property Institute (API), which can provide you with a list of registered valuers in your area.

A good valuer will have the appropriate qualifications; a valuer is not permitted to practise without a licence. In addition to that, membership of an industry-based association, such as the Australian Property

Institute (API), is important, as it provides ongoing training, contact and interaction with other property professionals, and a framework of ethics and valuation standards, principles and practice.

The land surveyor

A land surveyor is needed to determine and mark a property's boundaries. Using specialised equipment, a surveyor collects information and then uses the measurements gained to draft plans showing the exact layout of the block of land and where your proposed units will be.

A land surveyor is also needed if you want to subdivide your property. They will check if the land meets the requirements to be subdivided.

The advice and information a land surveyor provides helps you decide on the best use of your land for a prospective subdivision or development. The plans the surveyor draws up will be used by the rest of the team (engineer, architect, builder, and so on) as the basis for the building's design and construction, so that it best fits the space and the landscape. Any plans drawn up will also be submitted to council as part of the development application.

When choosing a land surveyor, select one who:

1. Has completed the necessary study to get their licence, and has years of professional experience. You will want to make sure they are licensed.

2. Has a thorough understanding of boundary law and the legal aspects of boundary surveying.

3. Has a reasonable turnaround time for the report – it usually takes one to two weeks from the visit to the site to the delivery of the report.

4. Charges a reasonable fee – to survey a property pegged for the development of two or three units, the cost is about $2,000 to $3,000.

Once you've chosen a surveyor, give them a copy of your title deed for the land. If you have any extra data, such as a previous survey, give the surveyor a copy of that as well. The surveyor will, after confirming all the information they have on site, provide a report on the size and dimensions of the lot, which you can use as part of your application to council.

The developer

Property development involves everything from the purchase, renovation and resale of existing buildings, to finding and buying land, and then subdividing, developing and on selling it to others at various stages of development. They may do this for their own portfolio or on a hire basis to a property owner.

Their work involves finding and then buying land to capitalise on its potential. This may be a vacant block or a site with established buildings. A developer will typically organise the entire process from acquisition to sales. Therefore, developers must bring a range of skills to the table that are usually acquired over the course of multiple years. While there are strong profits to be made from property development, there are also considerable financial risks involved as well. The investment in time alone is significant, as a rule of thumb a developer must look at 100 properties to put offers on 10 in hopes of acquiring 1!

With the land secured, the developer will then go about completing the seven steps which are the core of this book, either themselves or by outsourcing to other specialists.

In some markets, a developer will choose to specialise in a particular stage of the process. For example, a developer may buy land, then seek approval from the local council for subdivisions and permission to build. Once they have all the official paperwork completed, the developer can on sell the property, along with all the approved plans, to a builder at a premium price. Or the developer may choose to work strictly on the construction aspect of development, going so far as to hire his own team for the building rather than contracting it out to a third party. Some developers choose to focus on the management aspects of projects, making sure everything is in the right place at the right time and is costing the agreed amount.

When choosing a property developer, look for one who:

- Has completed no fewer than five projects.
- Is an expert at feasibility and budget plans and will be able to advise you of the best pathway to maximise profit and minimise risks.
- Has resolved issues with the property owner in a fair and open manner. There is nothing wrong with a developer having faced legal issues, as this is part of doing business. It is how they resolve those issues that make them stand out.
- Understands how to minimise the extra costs caused by delays.
- Has at least a couple of testimonials they can pass on to you for direct contact.

The architect or building designer

While engaging an architect sounds straightforward, the scope of what an architect can do for you varies greatly, as do the prices charged from professional to professional. Some projects can also be handled by building designers. So, before making a selection, it is worth investigating the difference between the two, the skills they bring to your project, and the range of costs that might be incurred for each.

An architect normally specialises in certain areas of building. New architects in the industry usually deal in home design, while more experienced architects are often involved in commercial, industrial and civil buildings. Any architect you work with should be registered with the Australian Institute of Architects. For an architect to legally use that title in Australia, they must be 'board registered'. If they're not, and something goes wrong with your project, you will not be able to hold them responsible, as they will have no insurance.

The architect's role is to help you determine the best use for a block of land and maximise your profit. Assuming the best use is multiple units on your block of land, the next tasks for the architect are to produce a concept design, help to set a viable and realistic budget, and produce detailed building plans which reflect that budget. Additionally, they can guide you through the town planning process, obtain competitive quotes for the work, manage consultants such as surveyors and engineers, monitor the budget and administer the construction contract, and so on. Your architect may inspect the actual work throughout the construction phase to ensure the quality and level of finishes you expect. Their fee is typically between three and six per cent of the construction cost or contract price of the work, until completion of the entire project. If the architect is contracted on a piece-by-piece basis for the project, each piece will have its own negotiated price.

A building designer is more commonly found in residential projects than an architect. Unlike architects, building designers do not need to hold a degree in architecture. However, many building designers have completed a number of years of architectural study.

Building designers are registered in Victoria, Queensland and Tasmania in the rest of the states they are accredited (versus registered), in both cases they are required to carry professional indemnity insurance and undertake continuing professional development. They provide the same services as an architect, but not necessarily to the same level. The architect completes a five-year course whereas a building designer completes a two-year course. For this reason, you can't expect that they will provide the same level of service. Their fees reflect both the lower licensing requirements (which vary from state to state) and, in some cases, the competency of the individual across the entire range of projects (individual homes, apartment buildings, public facilities, and so on). Their fees range from one to three per cent of construction cost or contract price.

You should choose to work with an architect or building designer who has developed property for themselves, or worked with builders or developers before on at least several similar projects and in a similar role. The reason for this is that they will understand the concept of undertaking a viable project that is reasonably affordable to build without compromising the quality.

The architect or building designer captures your ideas, then aligns them with council regulations to create plans and drawings, which your builder and other tradespeople can then follow to deliver a finished project to you. This includes:

- **Design consultation.** You may have taken advantage of one of these during your feasibility step to come up with best-use scenarios for the property. Here's an example of a site feasibility study, showing two different options for a block of land:

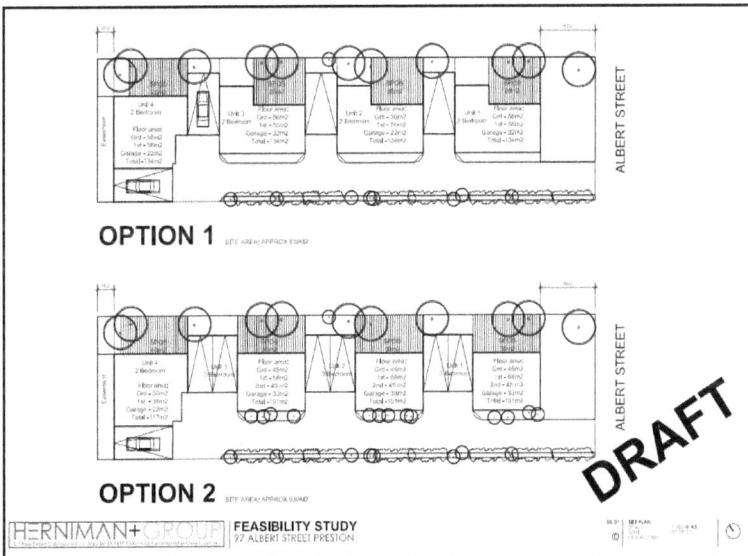

Source: Herniman + group

- **Access to their network of professional contacts.** When it comes time to bring in contractors to do the work, having access to a database of competent and fully insured tradespeople is vitally important in order for your project to be delivered on time and on budget.

- **Preparation of conceptual designs and drawings suitable for presentations.** Town planning and detailed drawings are a key element of securing finance (as they allow potential lenders to have a clear understanding and vision of what you are proposing), and also for gaining building permission from local councils.

- **Preparation of working drawings using drawing/architectural software applications.** These drawings and their accompanying specifications are put into the tender request (when you are looking to hire a builder or contractor) and into the council's review process of the development. They play an important role in establishing what the builder and other tradespeople will deliver. The more detailed the list and the drawings, the more likely it is that all parties will understand them.

- **Onsite supervision.** After engaging the rest of your team, you will need an onsite supervisor, and the architect will be able to help you secure one. They will ensure the work being performed, and materials being used, are in line with the necessary specifications, and comply with the terms and conditions of the contract.

It can be overwhelming choosing an architect for your project, especially if you've never done it before. Thankfully, there is a process you can follow.

1. **Understand your needs.** Begin by making sure you understand your needs for the project and be ready to describe them in as much detail as you can. What will you expect the architect to do? If you attempt to engage someone without first having a good idea of what they will be doing for you, that's a recipe for disaster.

2. **Determine your selection criteria.** Will you go with the cheapest architect, the most experienced, the busiest, the one with the best brochures, best testimonials, or insurance and bonds in place? In my view, getting a family member or friend to recommend someone is the best option.

3. **Utilise your network for referrals and recommendations.** Ask them what the scope of the work was that formed the basis for the referral. Always attempt to line up what a professional has done for other clients with what you want them to do.

4. **Check licensing agencies.** Go online and look at the licensing agencies or associations, and filter their list of members based on your needs.

   In each state and territory of Australia, it is a legal requirement that any person using the title 'architect', or offering services to the public as an architect, must be registered with the architects' board in that jurisdiction. Those agencies include:

   • NSW Architects Registration Board
   • Architects Registration Board of Victoria
   • Board of Architects of Queensland
   • Architectural Practice Board of South Australia
   • Architects Board of Western Australia

- Australian Capital Territory Architects Board
- Board of Architects of Tasmania
- Northern Territory Architects Board

5. **Get their background.** Review the time they have been in the market, their experience with the town planning council office in your area, and their website and testimonials. Check with the consumer authority in your state or territory for any complaints made against them, and Google them to track down additional comments about their work.

6. **Meet with your shortlist.** Create a shortlist of candidates and schedule a time to meet each of them. As a rule of thumb, the first meeting with them should be free of charge.

Capture the following information to help you make a decision on whom to hire:

- Contact information for their previous clients and the addresses of their past projects, which you should visit in person.

- How they have handled similar projects, what issues have they faced and how they dealt with them.

- Their availability to work on your project and their preferred start date.

- Whether the architect shares your vision of what should be built on the block or has a better idea.

- How they charge. Is it fixed fee or hourly? Always try to agree in a fix rate.

The next step is to create another, smaller shortlist, and develop and submit a request for a quote (also known as a request for proposal) to each of them.

When requesting quotes, make sure you set a realistic date (one to two weeks) by which you want to have the quotes returned. Make it clear to the architects that if they need more time, they should make contact with you to ask for an extension.

In order to make side-by-side comparisons of the quotes, draw up a simple table like this one. Along the top, list the different architects (A, B and C), and in the far-left column list the services they provide. Then fill in the remaining columns with the cost of each service, as quoted by each architect.

	Architect A	Architect B	Architect C
Architectural drawings	$5,000	$5,500	$6,000
Submission of application	$1,500	$2,000	$1,000
Town Planning	$1,000	$1,500	$1,200
Total	$7,500	$9,000	$8,200

Review the quotes against your predefined selection criteria, and then meet with the preferred architect to finalise and sign the contract.

The interior designer

An interior designer works with you to make all the rooms in your home both functional and attractive. They will first talk with you about your ideas for the final look of the home, your lifestyle and how various rooms will be used, and then put together a plan for the home in terms of colour selection and the style of any fixtures and fittings, based on your budget. Some architects have an in-house interior designer.

A designer can be useful in the design and planning stages of a project to optimise the layout of a room and how spaces can be used. By hiring an interior designer at the beginning, they can help you decide what kind of material you will use, and give you an idea of the costs involved.

An interior designer can also prove valuable when it's time to sell the property, or properties.

If you plan to sell the house once construction is completed, furnishing it (staging) is very important if you want to sell for top dollar. This gives potential buyers an indication of whether their furniture will fit inside the house, and also provides ideas on how to decorate the house.

Fortunately, you don't have to buy furniture to do this. An interior designer may be able to offer you a house-staging service. They hire furniture at a cost of $3,000 to $5,000 to stage the entire house, and it is only removed once the house has been sold.

When you are looking at engaging an interior designer, think about what you want to achieve visually and spatially, and look for a designer whose own style will complement your project. Research the kinds of projects they take on, and, if possible, try to view some of their previous work to get a good feel for the designer themselves.

It is also important to be upfront about what you can and can't afford. Some interior designers will charge hourly while others will charge an overall fee. The cost can vary depending on reputation and demand for that particular interior designer. Try to work with a designer who is transparent about costs, and don't be afraid to ask questions. If your designer charges by the hour, just remember that any time you engage their services, advice or opinions, you will generally be charged for this. Again, try to agree on a fixed price. As part of their compensation, interior designers also get commission from suppliers.

The quantity surveyor

A quantity surveyor (also known as a cost manager or construction economist) calculates the value of construction costs and labour for a building, beginning with the feasibility study and all the way through construction to completion.

A quantity surveyor provides advice on the most cost-effective way to achieve the desired result. Their data is used to provide estimates for the overall budget, and control costs and cash flow during the scope of work. During construction, a quantity surveyor will also be able to calculate the cost of any changes to design or quantity of materials.

After construction is completed, a quantity surveyor can also provide a depreciation schedule for tax purposes. This is used to claim any tax deductions you are entitled to if the property will be used to produce rental income.

Deductions in a depreciation schedule are with regard to the wear and tear of the property's structure known as 'capital works' (construction or installation of facilities and fixtures associated with, and forming an integral part of those works), as well as assets known as 'plant and equipment' contained within the property. The finalised schedule is then included in your tax return by your accountant.

The depreciation schedule also provides you with an estimated life for each asset, which is helpful for calculating when replacements or upgrades will be required, and also for getting home and contents insurance.

The building surveyor

A building surveyor is a licensed and insured professional whose field of expertise is in understanding building laws, codes and construction standards. A building surveyor is responsible for ensuring that the building is soundly built to existing building standards and, increasingly, are called upon to assess buildings' energy efficiency.

After a land surveyor has determined that you can build, a building surveyor can ensure that your building plans get council approval, guiding you through the development approval and building permit processes. After building commences, your building surveyor can also act as your building inspector throughout the building process and issue a certificate of compliance when construction is completed.

A building surveyor is engaged in public and private roles, and their field of expertise includes:

- Assessing, approving and inspecting building work.

- Assessing compliance with legislative requirements, approval of building and use changes, determining upgrades for existing buildings, building audits, compliance, and enforcement matters beyond the building approval process.

- Facilitating the regulatory approval process.

- Acting as a consultant on design, fire safety, energy efficiency and access solutions.

- Providing education and expert witness services in support of the legal process.

- Issuing relevant permits and approvals and undertaking enforcement.

The mortgage broker

A mortgage broker will show you a selection of the best rates, terms and conditions from both banks and other lenders for the project you are undertaking. Their services are usually free, as they get a commission from the bank for organising the loan. (This compensation is often included in the loan origination fee of between one and two per cent.) Some brokers will charge an upfront fee to help their client to get a construction loan for a development, as it requires much more time and effort from them than a traditional home loan application.

As such, it's a good idea to have them show you a full range of loan options, as some banks may pay a higher commission to the brokers to attract their business. The thing to remember is that, even though it's the bank paying a commission to the broker, there is a good chance that the bank will recover that money from you. It does this through the amount of interest you pay over the duration of the loan or origination/application fees.

Mortgage brokers have their finger on the pulse of the lending institutions and they are across the full lending market, including non-bank lenders that specialise in different types of funding. They know lending requirements, how much each financial institution will lend based on what type of property is being developed, how many units were pre-sold, what deposits were taken on those pre-sales, debt-to-equity ratios of the borrowers, and the type of equity being put up as collateral for the loan. They will be able to direct you to the best lender for your specific situation.

It is worthwhile putting together a professional-looking brochure to go with your concept drawings and financial documentation when you talk with the mortgage broker about financing. A brochure will make it a lot easier for the broker to find a lender on your behalf.

The brochure should include the following:

- An outline of the project.

- Site information – location, title, land size, and so on.

- Planning and building permit approval.

- Market report of the existing property and the properties to be developed.

- Demographics, statistics and growth of the area, including maps and photos of the site and neighbourhood, and three-dimensional images of the new units.

- Land surveyor report.
- Architectural drawings and specifications.
- Feasibility studies.
- Rental appraisal prepared by a property manager.
- Schedule of sales price, sales contract, and off-the-plan contracts prepared by a solicitor.
- Valuation of the land prepared by a property valuer.
- Profile and capability statement of the professional team.
- A list of the developer's past projects.
- Financial information and assets of the directors.
- Construction contract.

Lenders are looking to minimise their risk, which is normally based on the type of project you're undertaking, the number of pre-sales, your capability to repay debt, the experience and reputation of the developer, and the track record of the team. Based on the level of risk, the bank will negotiate the interest rate, upfront fees, the length of the construction loan, and the level of guarantees. The stronger your capability to repay the loan, the better your lending terms will be.

With the large number of brokers out there, it can be difficult to choose the right one. It's important that your broker has proven experience and a strong customer focus, so look for a broker with a long list of happy clients and repeat business.

With regard to credentials, ensure your broker is registered with the Australian Securities and Investments Commission, and has an Australian credit licence or is an authorised credit representative.

Also, be sure to find out their fee structure. Most brokers will provide their service for free, as they get paid a commission from the lenders (this commission should always be disclosed to you). Some brokers also charge a fee for service. This is usually a flat dollar fee.

The builder

A builder is responsible for the construction of your house, and must provide a warranty for the work they have done and materials they have used. As outlined in Section 1, Step 6, any builder you engage must have building insurance to protect you against defective and incomplete work.

The builder is the person who oversees the entire process of your home's construction, and they are your point of contact for anything you need during that time. The builder ensures that work is done on time and on budget, and also deals with building inspectors to demonstrate that all work is up to the standard required by the respective government codes and laws. They are also responsible for engaging and coordinating all the tradespeople needed for the build.

To find a builder, visit masterbuilders.com.au, which allows you to search for master builders in your area.

When hiring a builder, there is the option to have them work for a fixed price or costs plus fee.

A fixed price quote requires the builder to complete the work at a predetermined sum and within a certain time. You should keep any variations (extras) to a minimum as they can cause the price to rise and the construction to be delayed.

A costs plus fee means that the builder does not need to give the price at the start of the project. Instead, the homeowner agrees to pay for the work costs plus a fixed fee or a percentage of the total cost, usually between ten and fifteen per cent. The problem with using this type of contract is that you do not know the total cost of the project.

Considerations when selecting a builder include:

- Are they licensed?
- What is their history as a builder, including financial insolvency?
- Do they offer a certificate of currency for home indemnity insurance as part of their service (names of insurance types and coverage changes from state to state)?
- Can they commit to a start and end date?
- How do they deal with changes?
- How do they manage costs during the build and what do they do to avoid cost overruns?
- How do they manage inspections and sign-offs?
- How often is the builder actually on site (versus subcontractors)?
- Can they provide references?
- Do they quote on everything required for the build, including landscaping?
- Are there any other costs I am responsible for?

- What warranty do they offer for their work and materials and that of their subcontractors?

- What is the warranty period?

- Is the entire build covered by their insurance or are components omitted (e.g. foundations)?

- How do they commit to communicate with you during the build?

- How will payments for the project be made?

If the builder gives you a contract, show it to your solicitor before you sign it to get feedback and guidance on any clauses in the fine print that may be of concern.

The project manager

The project manager acts as the contact point for anyone involved in the construction phase of the house. Their role is to plan, coordinate, budget, manage and document all aspects of the construction to ensure it is completed on time and on budget.

The project manager is also in regular contact with you, the owner, to keep you updated on progress. In terms of home building, the project manager is often someone who is already involved in the project, such as the developer, architect or builder.

They will monitor budgets to compare estimates with final costs, and ensure that payment is only made once the work is completed. A project manager is available to give real-time updates on the progress of the project whenever you need them. In addition, they will send written reports on a regular basis. These reports outline the day-to-day progress of the project – what is done, what still needs to be done, when it will be done, how long it will take, how much it will cost, any material variations, any problem encountered in the project, and so on. Most importantly, the project manager will ensure there is open communication between everyone involved in the project.

Having an overview of the whole project allows the project manager to anticipate any problems that may arise in advance, and take steps to avoid or minimise them. They can also look for ways to save money on the project through optimising the use of resources.

If you decide to hire a project manager in addition to your architect and builder, ask to meet potential candidates on site for an interview. Make sure you bring any documents relevant to the build (plans, con-tracts, quotes, and so on) for them to look over.

Even many experienced developers engage project managers because a good project manager can save you a lot of money over the duration of the development.

A good project manager has excellent people and communication skills, a high degree of self-discipline and dedication to their work, and an ability to see the big picture.

Considerations when selecting a project manager include:

- How many projects will they handle simultaneously?
- What challenges have they seen and how did they deal with them?

- How do they monitor and control progress of a project?

- What steps do they recommend to maintain a high level of quality on the project?

- Have they ever had a project fail? Why, and what did they learn from it? (Problems are expected. The challenge is to overcome them and grow with the process. This is what you should be looking for in the project manager's answer.)

- What thoughts has the project manager shared with you regarding your project? What insights and lessons learned did they provide while on site?

- Can they provide local references? (Get the necessary information and call the referees.)

- What are their costs? (Normally two to five per cent of construction cost)

The engineer

In some circumstances, aspects of the home development may require you to work with an engineer. Easy to write but, as there are numerous engineers, you will really need guidance from your architect or building designer when deciding what engineering help you need and when. The following is a list of potential engineering professionals you might engage:

- Geotechnical/soil engineer: Normally engaged to test the soil composition and to design solutions for basements, footings and foundations.

- Structural engineer: Engaged to develop a structural design that is both functional and cost-effective. Normally engaged only when the construction requirements are unique or especially challenging.

- Civil engineer: Engaged most often by councils to design roads, bridges and other public work projects. Seldom required on a residential project.

- Acoustic engineer: Engaged where there is the need to reduce noise generated outside the residence from entering the residence, or isolating noise within the residence (e.g. home cinema, indoor gaming room).

- Hydraulic engineer: Engaged for all things water-related that may affect your residential construction or which may be affected by your development. Examples include waste water, rainwater and nearby natural water sources.

- Electrical engineer: Engaged when the residential construction calls for unusual or complex electrical solutions. Rarely required on normal residential projects.

Engineers focus on the stability and strength of the construction and how the building interacts with its environment: water run-off/drainage, hard surfaces versus permeable, complex underground building, etc. They ensure that the plans and the materials used contribute to the desired solution for which it has been designed.

The engineer will work in conjunction with the architect or building designer with regard to the design of structures and the materials specified, and provide a report summarising all of this information. Typically, it is up to the builder or architect to hire the engineer; the homeowner rarely interacts with them.

The landscaper

A landscaper helps put the finishing touches on a development once construction has been completed, ensuring the exterior of the home looks as good as the interior. Whether you are planning to sell the development or hold on to it for rental purposes, the presentation of the grounds helps to maximise the return on your investment.

It is very important to choose plants which look good but don't break your budget. A lot of homeowners want their garden – particularly their front garden – to be visually stunning. You can achieve that without having to spend a lot of money. A talented landscape architect will be able to choose the best plants for your budget. Much depends on the statement you are trying to make (commonly referred to as kerbside appeal) and council requirements.

Most councils have a specific set of landscape design guidelines. For example, the City of Manningham refers to 'functional considerations' in landscape design, including:

- The location of outdoor living areas, service paths, water tanks, retaining walls, decks, sheds and bin storage.
- Suitable grading of paved areas, lawns and garden beds.
- Selection of plants in regard to the site conditions.
- Responding to microclimate conditions (sun, shade, dry, wind).
- Providing mature heights and spreads of proposed planting.

In addition to grading and levelling the site, planting trees and shrubs, and laying grass, a landscaper can also repair outside areas which may have been damaged during the construction of the new dwelling, such as erosion caused by heavy rain. Other services they can provide include laying paving for paths, patios and driveways, building garden features like pergolas, and installing irrigation systems for ongoing maintenance of the garden.

Normally, the architect will be able to refer a landscape designer. Local recommendations are always a good choice to review as well.

Before meeting with the landscaper, make a list of the features you want in the areas surrounding the house, and ask for feedback as to their suitability. Based on your ideas, the landscaper will then come up with designs for your approval.

The arborist

An arborist is trained in the field of planting, caring for and removing trees. Generally, they will be sourced by the architect or landscape designer.

The correct treatment of trees can add significant value to your development. Poorly maintained trees can be a liability, as well as dangerous. An arborist can identify if a tree is healthy or dead, and if it can cause harm to other residents. Monitoring or removing trees and working at height requires training and accreditation, as you could be dealing with factors such as power lines, wildlife, and nearby fences or homes. When dealing with trees on a mature block of land, the arborist is usually the one to help convince the council that it is okay to remove a tree or how to protect an existing tree (yours or your neighbours) during demolition and construction.

Ask the arborist to do a site inspection of the property, and have any drawings done by the builder or architect available for them to review, in order to give them a clear picture of the work you want done. Compare their fees and estimated costs for infrastructure, soil and plants with one or two others.

"Teamwork makes the dream work, but a vision becomes a nightmare when the leader has a big dream and a bad team."
- John C. Maxwell

It is a long journey, but it's worth it

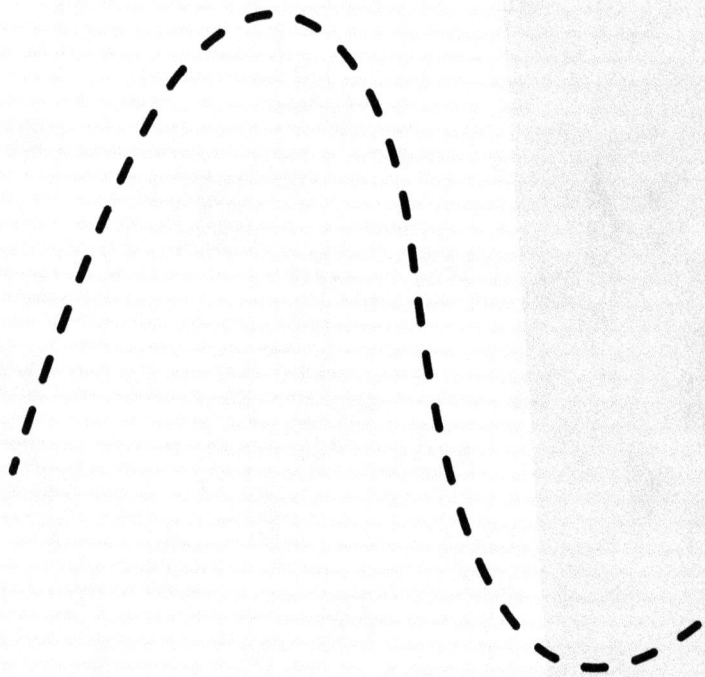

INTERVIEWS WITH THE PROFESSIONALS

All of the information you need about subdividing and developing your property can be found in Sections 1 and 2. However, sometimes it helps to hear directly from the experts. That's why I've included Section 3, featuring interviews with seven professionals who are instrumental in the subdivision and development process. Hopefully, these additional insights will prove useful as you embark on your own property development journey.

AN INTERVIEW WITH REAL ESTATE AGENT ANTHONY GUNN

✗- - - - - - - - - - -

Iva: **Anthony, would you please tell me a bit about yourself?**

Anthony: I'm a real estate agent and have been for twenty-eight years. My father was a prominent builder in Melbourne for many years also, so I know building sites. I've had a lot of experience with investors looking to create wealth and I also manage a substantial portfolio, and we sell quite a lot of real estate.

I've worked within two large network franchise organisations with offices in Melbourne, so I've had good experience in dealing with clients in different suburbs.

Iva: **How does a homeowner find out the end value of their property? Do they need a rough design or full, detailed drawings?**

Anthony: If somebody is looking at constructing a unit in their backyard, they should engage a designer to come up with a rough sketch plan that will meet the intent of the good design guide and will be constructed to allow for the right amount of private open space per dwelling. It should also allow for proper vehicular access and garaging or carports. It should be a proper sketch, drawn to scale, with perhaps a front elevation so that the prospective developer can speak to a couple of real estate agents to understand what the likely resale value of that parcel of land with a new design should realise.

So, we can estimate resale value pretty easily by looking at comparative sales data out in the marketplace. The agent looks at home size, land area and how the design will orientate on the site, and what sort of natural light will be in the property. Having drawings of the front elevation design would also help in understanding what it's going to look like. The agent can also offer advice on whether they think the design is suited to the area.

Agents are good to talk to because they're generally abreast of the market trends in an area. A lot of times, people come to see me with designs that they think might sell well, whereas in fact we believe that they might not be the right local style for that particular market or area. Sometimes, people squeeze so much onto the site, which makes the design clunky and overbearing for the amount of land. Other times, people design something that's not the right size and underutilise the land as well. So again, talking to a good agent – who has a footprint in the local marketplace – can help avoid problems later on.

Iva: **When should someone engage with a real estate agent if they are thinking about subdividing their property?**

Anthony: I believe from the very start, because, again, agents can offer advice on what is selling well for that area. They will also provide invaluable advice on things like building two townhouses side by side but without the constraints of shared driveways. This is because once you start putting shared driveways on these sites, we have to create an owners' corporation situation, which a lot of people are not happy with, and, as a result, the homes can be a little bit harder to sell as a lot of people don't like sharing driveways.

My feeling is that a lot of people do prefer to have larger townhouses ... They sell for more money. They are easy to build if they're side by side. So, an agent can assist you in creating a design that's going to work for that specific market.

Iva: **Following construction, how should an owner or developer select the real estate agent to sell their property?**

Anthony: Experience is a major factor, and having a proven track record in the area. I would always engage an agent who has good ethics and a footprint in the marketplace. Not necessarily the biggest agency – that doesn't guarantee the best result. Most importantly, don't overpay. Pay what's fair in the marketplace by checking the going rates with two or three local agencies ... You should interview agents, understand what their core strengths are, and make your own assessment.

Iva: **If the owner or a developer wants to hold and rent their property, do they need a different professional?**

Anthony: No. Any good real estate agency will have several divisions of their business for sales and rentals ... An agency that doesn't have a rental division is not really taking the job seriously.

Iva: **What are the fees involved in managing a rental property?**

Anthony: There's generally a management fee and a letting fee. So, when we let a property, we put a board up and advertise it on the internet. We get professional photography done to showcase the property in its best light. The management fee is generally negotiable, somewhere between five per cent and seven per cent of the rental amount.

Iva: **How are agents compensated for their initial assistance?**

Anthony: When people contact a real estate agent, if the agent is not prepared to invest some pretty serious time in assisting people and getting them started in the right direction, that agent is probably not here for the long haul.

So [good real estate agents are] here for the long haul, happy to give free advice, and provide people with contact details of good people that can assist with the design process. Then it is a case of letting people go off and make their own decisions on what they want to do.

Iva: **How is the agent compensated for the sale of the property?**

Anthony: If somebody goes through the design process and the agent has done everything right, and assisted by helping them find a builder and build something, we will simply charge a marketing fee and a commission to sell that property in accordance with all the normal sales processes.

Iva: **How would an off-the-plan sale enter into the owner's or developer's strategy?**

Anthony: What I like most is that the builders will allow people who buy early in the process to be modestly flexible with the internal fixtures and fittings. People have the chance to personalise the design through such things as upgrading the wall oven, and so on. So, to my way of thinking, offering to sell the property in the initial stages helps the buyer to save money and have some input into what's constructed.

Iva: **Any success stories you'd like to share?**

Anthony: One of our clients owned two parcels of land next door to each other. We introduced them to a really good builder who built one townhouse free of charge for them, and his payment was the second townhouse he built on the other parcel of land on the same allotment. As it was, the owner could have sold the existing property for $1.3 million, but the builder created and designed a really amazing townhouse. We did sell one of them off the plan for $1.65 million, so that's a really good outcome. That person ended up with a very substantial double-storey townhouse that's worth far more money than their original weatherboard house.

Iva: **Anything else you'd like to add?**

Anthony: Talk to a building designer. Understand what can be constructed on the land. Don't try and reinvent the wheel or design something that's not suited to the area. That's why you need to speak to agents. If you stick to that advice, the planning process should run a lot smoother and you'll get a better outcome. That will take a lot of the stress out of the process.

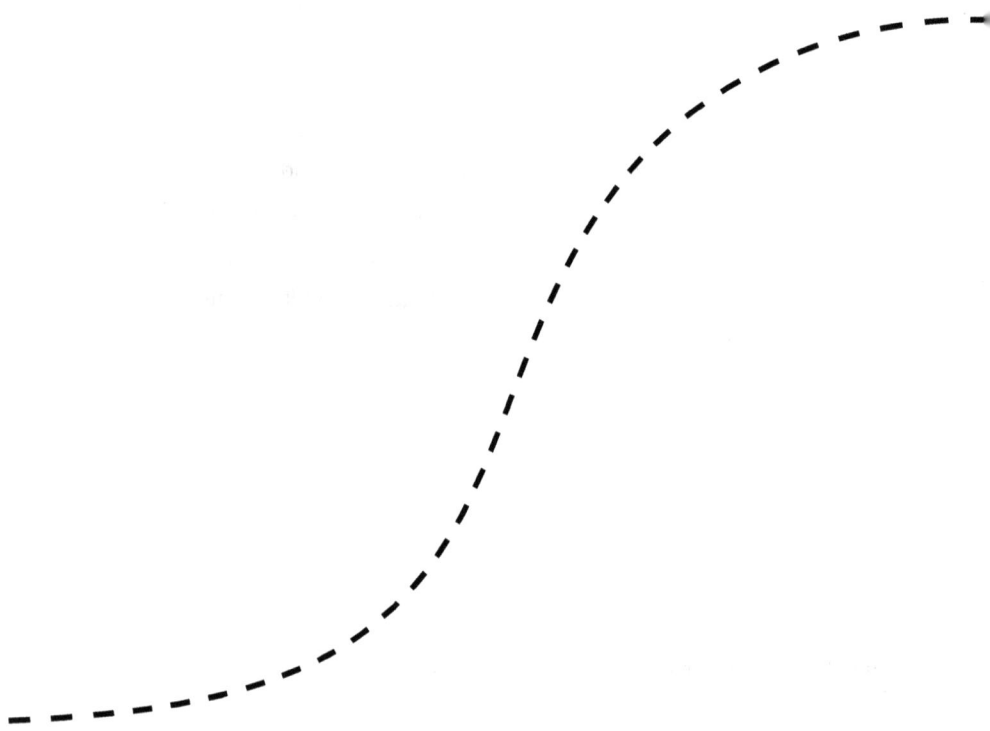

AN INTERVIEW WITH LAND SURVEYOR JEREMY PEARCE

— — — — — — — — — — ✕

Iva: **Jeremy, please tell us about yourself.**

Jeremy: I'm a licensed land surveyor with thirty years of experience ... I'm licensed by the state of Victoria to perform title surveys ... We assist people measuring and mapping their land, subdividing their land, and transacting changes to the boundaries of their land.

Iva: **How can you help a person who wants to subdivide their land?**

Jeremy: A licensed land surveyor must be involved in the transactions of changes in lands, [and] that includes subdivision or amendments of the boundary. We can assist with title surveys, first of all determining the relationship with your fences to your title, and can also be involved with your designer to come up with proposed boundaries for those plans. We also make applications to council to assist subdivision of the land.

Iva: **At what stage do you become involved in a project?**

Jeremy: For a typical two-lot subdivision, we're involved at the earliest stage. We do a title survey, determining if there are any encroachments on the property by others around it. [We're] measuring and mapping the title, possibly the house, as well as all the windows, vegetation, land forms, drainage, points of service locations for servicing a proposed lot, right through to the final design and application to the council for the subdivision.

Iva: **Are you involved in the construction as well?**

Jeremy: Yes, we do assist with a set-out of the structures. We'll take the working drawings from the designer and mark the ground to assist setting the right position of the new dwellings.

Iva: **What fees do you charge?**

Jeremy: The fee structure is dependent on the situation, both legal and physical, that we have on the ground. We depend a lot on 'line of sight', so for a heavily vegetated lot, the price will be a little more than a clear lot. Also, if there's recent survey information, it's going to be cheaper than if we're following a survey from 100 years ago. That was done on horseback. So, our price to have title re-establishment is around $1,400 before GST. Our feature level survey is around $1,600 before GST, and subdivision is around $3,000 before GST for a two-lot subdivision.

Iva: **What about if it is more than two lots being subdivided? Does the price increase?**

Jeremy: There's a price increase of around $400 per lot but there's other complexities, such as the need for cross-sections to satisfy the land titles office when we start talking about multi-storey under overlapping entitlements. Some plans in subdivision get reasonably complex, with multiple cross-sections required.

Iva: **In what timeframe should the homeowner expect everything to be done by?**

Jeremy: There are two levels of subdivision applications you can make to the council for a permit to subdivide. One is the traditional form, whereby it's referred to authorities (servicing authorities, such as water, as well as gas, telecommunication and electricity authorities) for their comments and all of the authorities will reply, and the council will prepare a permit. That typically takes two to three months to receive that permit.

Iva: **How long does it take to complete your part of the service?**

Jeremy: It's a common question and the answer is as long as it takes the owners to satisfy the permits from council. What I mean by that is that there will be permit conditions issued by council for the subdivision. Unfortunately, I'm not in control of how quickly those are complied with, but we look to assist the client to satisfy those as quickly as possible. But some of them depend on the construction phases, so it's really about mapping a path right through to satisfy a permit condition in the quickest possible time. Most subdivisions will achieve the permit in two to three months and can be completed in six months, and nine months for most two- or three-lot subdivisions.

Iva: **So the process is get the planning permit first, then subdivide and then build. Is that correct?**

Jeremy: Yes, you can do that. A number of councils, though, have now introduced planning scheme amendments where you can subdivide land but you must have a valid permit to develop the land. Both planning permits have a distinction for development, which permits the building of the second dwelling, as opposed to subdivision, which is a planning permit for the division of the land.

Iva: **What are your recommendations for someone who wants to subdivide and develop their backyard?**

Jeremy: First of all, consider if it's possible through the local planning schemes. To do this, you may need advice from a surveyor or a planner. What is your property zone? What is allowed on that zone? After investigating these things, talk to an architect, perhaps have someone to give some ideas of concepts, and then engage professionals as appropriate.

Iva: **What about due diligence? How can a land surveyor assist homeowners with that?**

Jeremy: A professional who has experience in these types of developments can have knowledge of possible pitfalls, which may not be obvious at the start. It would be wise to discuss with them the potential of the land and what pitfalls may occur.

Iva: **How much would this service cost?**

Jeremy: A regular suburb and block consultation is about $350 before GST.

Iva: **In your opinion, at what stage should a homeowner engage a land surveyor?**

Jeremy: Very early in the process because we lay down the context while the other people design. We provide information about clearance to an existing dwelling and a title survey, combined with a feature level survey, which provides the context for the designer to work from. We also advise what can fit in with council regulations, and provide the backbone of the documentation required for the development permit and subdivision permit.

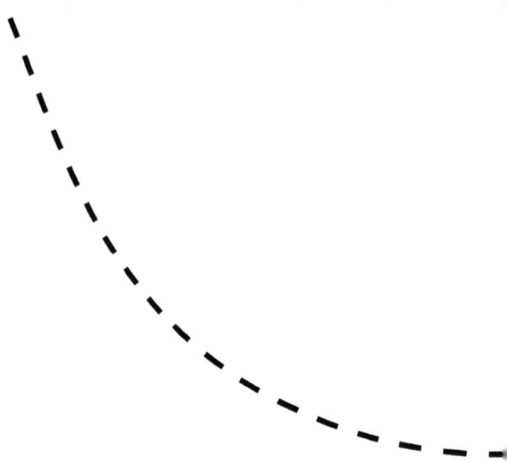

AN INTERVIEW WITH PROPERTY DEVELOPER ANDREW LENOX

— — — — — — — — — — —X

Iva: **Andrew, please tell me about yourself.**

Andrew: I started off as a developer in 2003 with a family block of land. We didn't have much money to spend or much knowledge on how to develop. All we knew is we had a great block of land because of everything that was getting developed around us. So, I went to speak with the council, land surveyors and town planners as a very inexperienced person about what ended up being a thirty-one-unit development.

As a result of this first project, I ended up getting a good team of people. I had a great design site and also had to create stuff, but I had people around me that could point me in the right direction. Within a little bit of time, I thought I could do this for other people because I've got such a great team. That was twelve years ago.

Iva: **What do you recommend for the homeowner thinking about subdividing and developing their backyard?**

Andrew: First of all, make sure it's profitable. I'm not saying that as a greedy developer; I'm saying that so you're not wasting time. If it's not profitable, the bank won't support you. If it's not profitable, you'll lose sleep. So, if you're in areas where the values are so low, I say don't do it. Wait or, if you've got the money behind you, you can hold [the property] for ten years.

'Is it realistic?' is the next question because there are a lot of people who aren't realistic and they spend a lot of money to ultimately find out they can't do what they hoped that they could do.

Iva: **In our book, we recommend the homeowner first goes to the council to find out what can be done on their property. Do you agree?**

Andrew: Yes, a council is set up so a homeowner can get advice over the counter.

Iva: **So what questions should they ask the town planner?**

Andrew: First of all, are they allowed to develop? ... You might think you've got a big backyard and it's quite easy to do, but you might have a native tree in the backyard which will completely change everything.

The other thing is the trees of your neighbours, because you may be able to pull your tree down but the next-door neighbour's tree may impact your development and you can't touch it.

Iva: **When the homeowner wants to apply for a planning permit, how do you help them with this step?**

Andrew: Well, there are a few people that get involved in a planning permit. So as a bare minimum, you need a land surveyor, a designer and a town planner. Now, legally you don't have to have a town planner. A lot of designers will do their own town planning reports, but I've rarely come across any designer who can do as good a job as a town planner. Remember, we're submitting an application to a town planning department. So, having a town planner involved is very important. They tie the process together.

So, our company does everything. But doing it alone, you would potentially just have the designer run the process. If it was me, I'd engage a town planner and they would engage the building designer and the land surveyor, but ninety per cent of the industry would engage a draftsman or a designer. They would get the land survey and liaise a little bit with the town planner. Essentially, they get the town planner at the end where they should be getting the town planner from the start. You can engage them all separately but you say, 'Hey, here's the team everyone. Town planner, you drive it.'

Iva: **What are the permits required for subdivision, planning and building? Are there others needed for things like tree removal and exceptions to the regulations?**

Andrew: Without complicating it, I'll say there are three permits you need. The first is town planning, the second is for building, and the third is for subdivision. Now, within each of these, you'll have smaller permits. For example, you'll need to get a demolition permit but that can be built into a construction contract. You don't need permits to remove trees because that will all be covered as part of the town planning. Sometimes, you'll have to get a build over easement permit, but they're all really part of the town planning [permit], building permit or the subdivision permit. So, we call it major permits and minor permits: Three major permits and then multiple small permits. So that's why we say you should engage a firm that can deal with all the permits.

Iva: **Who are the other professionals needed to carry out the subdividing and developing?**

Andrew: The most important thing with ongoing and successful property development is having a great team ... Every time you deviate from the team, you've got a new process to work out. So, if you've got a great team of people, then they should be dealing with a lot of this stuff that comes up.

Iva: **So when you have a client, would you recommend certain professionals?**

Andrew: Absolutely. We just give a client one contract and we cover every item. So, we would recommend a designer who would recommend an engineer who would recommend a soil tester who could recommend a land surveyor. So those three main people (designer, engineer and land surveyor) will be making recommendations to you. By having one contract, you just tell them to do it so it's not your problem.

Iva: **Do you have any insight on how to select these professionals?**

Andrew: If they haven't done unit development, don't be the guinea pig because you will suffer. If they're a one-man show, yes, they'll be cheaper. But by the time they get around to your project, they'll be two months slower than someone who's better, and your holding costs for two months will be $5,000 to $7,000. So now, they're more expensive.

As property developers, we engage good people – who know what they're doing – to protect your profits and your outcomes. So, my advice is don't go to the cheapest person … Get someone who has done this before because they're playing with your profits. Don't look at just how cheap they are. Look at your end profit margins, because, if they can do something better, then it's cheaper [in the long run]. As a result, your resell value will go up and that means more profit. Profits don't come from just discounts; profits come from an overall package and design.

Iva: **As a property developer, would you be involved in demolition and construction?**

Andrew: Our group does everything. We do one contract for construction, and it includes subdivision and demolition. A lot of builders won't want anything to do with demolition, and most builders want nothing to do with subdivision … Once again, if you can get your professionals to deal with it, you'll sleep much better.

Iva: **How frequently would you be in contact with your home-owner?**

Andrew: We say as a bare minimum, fortnightly. We're dealing with a lot of money and a lot of stress, so we have to keep the homeowners in the loop. Sometimes, there are problems on site. Typically, what we do is we fix problems before we tell the homeowner. We don't like to hit the homeowner with problems because they've engaged us to take away that stress ... We've also got online systems where the homeowner gets automatic updates.

Iva: **When do you move on? What event signals that your contribution to the project has ended?**

Andrew: When you pay your final bill! Actually, you would never hand over that final money until the occupancy permit was done. However, there is also a handover process where the homeowner will come in and approve everything. So, if there are any little defects, they have to be fixed. There's actually a maintenance period then. So, you're not expected to understand fully that everything is perfect when you move in. Sometimes, it might take you a week to find out that a tap doesn't work. So, builders have usually thirty, sixty or ninety days to find out if there's any defects while you're living there, and then the builder has to come back and fix them. Little defects aren't structural; they are cosmetic things (the toilet seat doesn't close properly, the bathroom door doesn't stay shut, the shower is dripping, and so on). So, the cosmetic period is thirty to ninety days, and the structural one, by law, is seven and a half years, but this is from the time the construction starts.

Iva: **Any horror stories or any success stories you'd like to share?**

Andrew: A client came to us with a great site and didn't realise how good it was. We looked at it and saw some extra potential.

The client paid approximately $1.7 million for this site. We got a town planning permit for a ten-storey building with a medical centre, and he sold with the plans and permits soon after for $3.4 million. So, in twelve months, we helped him make a $1.5 million profit for a $50,000 outlay for town planning. We look for things that other people don't see and we try to make great sites out of good sites.

Where the horror stories come from is when you have designers who don't really know what they're doing and who are trying to make profits that are just not there. People spend a year and a half and $20,000 on a development that won't go ahead.

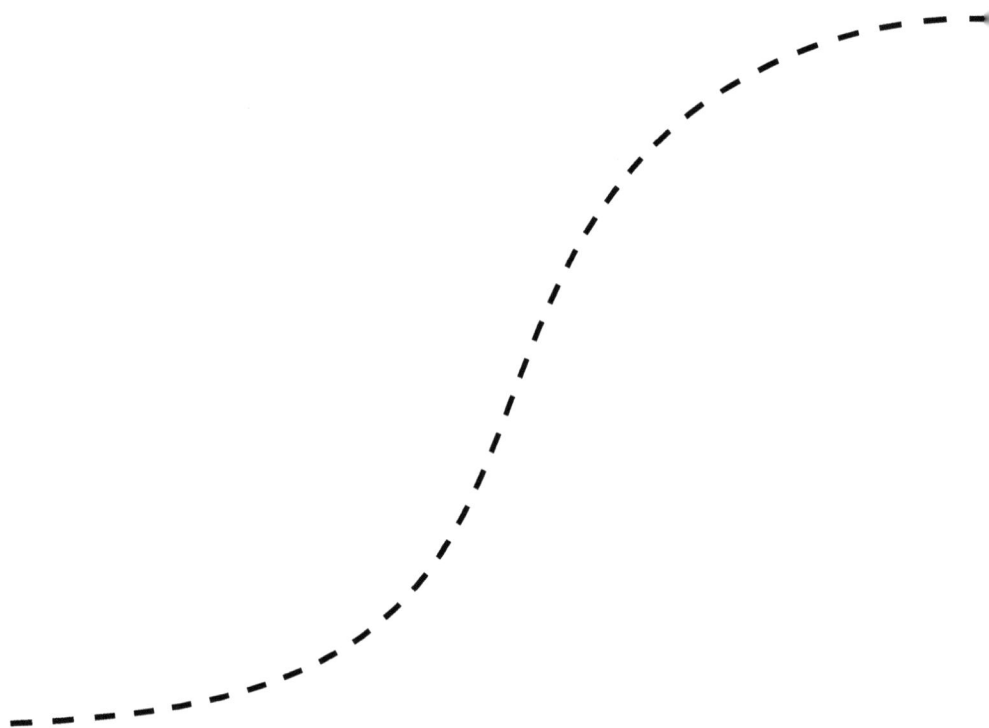

AN INTERVIEW WITH ARCHITECT JOHN HERNIMAN

------------ X

Iva: **John, please tell us a little bit about your background.**

John: I've been an architect for a long time. I started doing a lot of houses for people and then I gradually ... grew bigger. We do a lot of unit and apartment developments, but we also do aged care and hospitality [venues]. But I really like the personal touch when it comes to residential work.

Iva: **We have developed a seven-step approach to assist home-owners considering subdividing their backyard. I'd like to get your insight on when homeowners should engage an architect, and what specifically the architect will do for them.**

John: It's important to make sure you meet the marketplace and that the advice you get is really good at the start. We have to get permits. It's all to do with making sure that for the planning permit we achieve, we've reduced the risk on it, and any problems in the process are solved to get the permit as seamlessly as possible. So, you should ask the architect when you're just starting to think about whether it's a good idea [to subdivide] or not.

Iva: **Is it possible for homeowners to subdivide their block by themselves?**

John: If it's their first time, I think they're going to really struggle. You need somebody – it could be a town planner, surveyor or architect – to advise you as to whether you can do that. I can find out a lot about a property using a couple of websites that I know really well. Doing it on your own, I think that's fraught with danger.

Iva: **What is the value added by the architect?**

John: For any professional, you've got to be able to see that they've multiplied the value of the project by two or three times the cost of their fees, and have them demonstrate that. Otherwise, why would you bother? The other thing is making sure that we get the right value for the end product, and that we reduce the risk. That is the critical component of obtaining permits.

Iva: **How does someone gauge an architect?**

John: It's good to know the architect first, if you possibly can. Somebody who's got a track record in this space and it's a successful one ... You [should] get advice before you even go to council.

Iva: **I know the architect estimates total cost but, at the preliminary point of the project, do you have enough elements to do a cost?**

John: Very much so. We break it up into stages. The first stage is just to do a feasibility study of what you can fit on the site, how many units, and the number of square metres per unit. At that point, you can multiply the square metre by the construction rate per square metre, and that does the area cost.

For example, if the total construction cost per square metre (the estimate rate) is $1,500, and the number of square metres per unit is 150, you will multiply 150 x $1,500 to find the total construction cost of each unit which is equal to $225,000.

The architect needs to be very experienced to interpret that.

You also have to remember that you'll probably be demolishing things, and you need to be very careful of your neighbours' foliage and various planning overlays. You need to take all that into account in the feasibility [study].

Iva: **If the block of land conforms to council regulations and the real estate agent paints a positive picture, what's the next step after the design and costing?**

John: The next step is to get a surveyor to visit the site and to take levels, and do a feature survey of the surrounding area. That will be part of the drawings that are later lodged with council. We also, at that point, do drawings sufficient in quality to be able to go back to council. So, we have the bones of the original idea and convert it into drawings, where you know exactly where everything is located and, crudely, what it's going to look like.

So, we then go to council to get feedback. It's called a pre-application meeting, where council will tell you if your design has any issues, and invites you to upgrade the drawings before going back to council for a formal submission.

After going to council, we always sit down with a real estate agent and go back through the design with them, and upgrade their estimate of sale price so our client can redo their financial spreadsheet.

Iva: **How does an architect contribute to this step?**

John: An architect makes sure the client understands, right at the start, what the construction costs are likely to be and works to get it within a ballpark range. It will vary quite a lot, depending on the suburb, but the construction costs are relatively consistent. So, getting the feasibility [study completed] at the start is fantastic and it has to be done. The architect also makes sure the feasibility studies continue through into the design process and that the drawings, design, look of the building, and how it works, is efficient and looks good. This is done so that you get the next level of feedback and to ensure it fits into the marketplace outlined by the real estate agent. So, you could say that the architect is the conductor of the orchestra and pulls all these various factors together into a design that functions for the client. It's not a hero design for awards and things. It's a functional, right-looking building that works and is good for the client.

Iva: **So an architect will be able to do a feasibility study for a client?**

John: Certainly. I like my clients to understand the numbers and I really like clients who have done the feasibility themselves. It's important they understand the various ramifications of building cost versus sale price. We already know roughly what the land price is, so the other two factors are critical. A feasibility study should include everything: The architect's, surveyor's and engineer's fees, and also interests (for the loan, referred to as carrying costs).

Iva: **How are you compensated for this work?**

John: We're paid first on a phase-based [structure] or a fixed fee for each stage, and also by having a delighted client who wants to do it again.

Iva: **What other professionals should be called upon to contribute?**

John: It will vary but initially, it's the land surveyor who will do the survey at the start before we lodge with council. Then it's up to us to take it all the way through until it is actually lodged with council.

When it comes to the other professionals, sometimes we need a town planner but it's pretty rare at the scale we're talking about; that's usually only happening at the larger scale projects. When it comes to construction drawings, you will need an energy rater to rate the various energy issues, a landscaper, architect, a structural engineer and a civil engineer. (Civil engineers design systems to help cope with heavy periods of rain and water retention on site. For a residential property, a civil engineer may not be necessary.)

Iva: **When are the detailed construction plans created?**

John: Immediately after you've obtained [the] planning permit.

Iva: **Does an architect create everything? What is included in those plans?**

John: The interiors. The architectural blueprint for the building itself is set by the planning permit, but the interiors are not ... We have interior designers in our business who do all those drawings as they know what is appropriate. So, for high-value areas, they're more detailed with more expensive finishes, and a lower-valued area is the reverse. Also, we choose finishes, fittings, fixtures and the specifications as well. We coordinate all that with the structural engineer and the civil engineer and, along the way, make sure that the landscape is done as well. Sometimes, that's left as a separate contract though.

Iva: **Would you be involved during the demolition and construction? If so, how frequently would you be in contact with the homeowners?**

John: Clients quite regularly choose not to use architects during construction. They try and save money. I think if you're not used to doing it, you should hire the architect to project-manage.

When it comes to demolition, we like the builder to do the demolition, pull out the redundant services and do the construction – all in one package. It's easier to finance and makes one person responsible.

Iva: **Who handles the council inspection?**

John: That's the domain of the building surveyor who does inspections at particular stages. We do it more frequently

– on average, about once a week. Less at the start, more at the end, to make sure the quality is there.

Iva: **At the end of construction, how does the council let the homeowner know that the building is ready for occupation?**

John: There are two stages to that. One stage is when the building surveyor signs off. To sign off, it's not just the inspection of the buildings. It's making sure that the plumbing and the electrical have certificates. He checks all that and then issues an occupancy certificate. That goes to the various authorities and the owner of the building. The owner can then hand over those documents to the agent and the lawyer when they decide to sell, and they're part of the selling documents.

Iva: **When do you move on? What event signifies that your contribution is at an end?**

John: When you have the occupancy certificates, when anything you've got to sell is sold and settled or rented out, and you've taken a nice holiday to make up for all the stress.

Iva: **Any success stories that you'd like to share?**

John: I'd say that probably ninety-eight per cent of our stories are successful. In the last twelve months, we've had four projects that have gone to us because other professionals have not had what it takes to get the planning permit. We hate that because we have to retrace their steps with councils and get them on side again. But it goes to prove that you really do have to know what you're doing to get it done properly. Apart from being really good at designing great buildings, you've also got to be hard-headed when it comes to the business side of architecture.

AN INTERVIEW WITH ACCOUNTANT JOHN LOMBARDO

✗– – – – – – – – – – –

Iva: **John, please tell me about yourself and the different ways you have been involved in real estate.**

John: I've been an accountant for more than twenty-five years. Effectively, what I found was, as part of my role, I got involved about ten years ago into financing property. Real estate is a good avenue to invest in and create wealth long term. Also, you can utilise the tax laws in terms of negative gearing or claiming deductions through depreciation.

So, I decided to invest into property and also developed some properties and utilized that to create my asset base and wealth a little bit faster.

Iva: **How can an accountant help a homeowner?**

John: They help to review where your properties are at. If it's for investment, it's in terms of whether the investment is working and what tax benefit you're getting from that property. I also do finance, which is looking at how you get the best deal for the amount of finance you've got against the property, and are you getting the best rates and factors relating to that? So, I can marry both of those to make sure they're working, because, day to day, you find that lenders and banks are offering different rates and specials. So, what would have been good one year, the next year may have changed. That means you may need to review and get a better deal.

Iva: **At what point should a homeowner engage an accountant?**

John: Right at the very start if the homeowner's planning [on] subdividing a property, selling, or even if they're buying. I'll look at the consequences in terms of whether there are any capital gains implications for subdividing. Then I'll estimate what they're going to pay for subdivision, planning, council requirements, land surveys, etcetera. Then they will know what they may gain and what taxes could be liable on those gains.

It's the same thing if they were buying. I'll let them know, based [on] what they've spent, what the potential tax liability would be. That can be estimated upfront, so then you know what your inflows and your outflows are for an entire purchase, sale or subdivision early on. By doing this, there are no surprises down the track. People should always have an understanding of the overall strategy and how it will work within a framework for taxation and finance, in terms of any legal requirements they need to disclose.

Iva: **Do you work with financial planners, tax advisers and solicitors?**

John: I'm a financial planner, mortgage broker and a real estate agent. I decided to get qualifications in those areas so I can understand all aspects of the process my client wil be going through. But I deal with solicitors and conveyancers to make sure the legal transactions are done correctly.

Iva: **How should a homeowner select an accountant?**

John: It should be based on a number of things. Does the accountant have all the qualifications? (You can visit www.tpb.gov.au to check if they are registered.) How long have they been in business for? Does the accountant specialise in the same sort of things that I'm looking to do in terms of investing in property?

You also need to be comfortable with your accountant. There's no point having them say, 'Here's your tax return,' and not understand what's going on. I will explain how it all works and share my knowledge. So that way, the homeowner is empowered and understands what they're doing.

Iva: **What sorts of taxes are involved in subdividing and developing a backyard?**

John: The main tax would be capital gains. So, if you were to subdivide a backyard and then sell off the new section, capital gains tax would apply. The way it works is if it's your own home, then it's your own investment and it's exempt. However, the subdivided portion is treated under tax laws as a capital gains event. So, you would need to calculate what that backyard was worth out of the original purchase price. If it was purchased after September 1985, it is subject to capital gains. If it was purchased before September 1985, and you subdivided it, then there's an exemption.

So, if you bought in 2000 and you subdivided the backyard off in 2016, then you'd have to attribute a cost to that subdivided portion and then subtract that figure from the price you sold the backyard for, less any other costs you spent to prepare the land for sale. The difference is the gain, and that is what you would pay tax on.

For example, if you subdivided the backyard and sold it for $200,000, and the cost of that portion of the back-yard was calculated as being worth $100,000 and you had costs of $20,000 to subdivide it, then you'd have a gain of $80,000.

But the way capital gains [tax] works at the moment is that if you own the subdivision for more than twelve months, you get a fifty per cent discount, which cuts your gain to $40,000. Then you pay tax on that amount at your marginal tax rate. So, if it's 32.5 per cent, you'll pay $13,000 tax on an $80,000 profit.

Iva: **Is there any GST to be paid?**

John: If you're a developer and you're building a property and a home, then you could attract GST on the sale. Because the way GST works on property, and developing property for re-sale, is that if you sell a property that's developed and is less than five years old, the tax department would expect GST to be paid on the sale of that property. [With] any established properties or properties older than five years, or properties that you haven't developed, GST is not applicable.

Now, there's also a thing called margin scheme, which says that if the land a new property has been built on did not have GST applied on it, then that margin of GST that would have been payable on that land can come off the GST applicable to the sales price.

Iva: **So, can you help a homeowner to do feasibility?**

John: Yes, I've done spreadsheets that work on negative gearing and if a homeowner's buying a property to keep or to rent. So, for a feasibility of a subdivide property, I'd work out what price the homeowner was going to get, how much it's costing them and what the attributed value of the land is, to get an idea of the end result that they'd get. Then, assuming they'll keep their existing home, I would also calculate what the value of that would be.

Let's say you have an established front house and you build on the back. I have found that the value of the front house, even after you subdivide, is fairly close to what it was worth before you took away the block on the back. So, what we find is that you increase your total net worth, but obviously you need to seek a valuation to assess what the value is before and after.

Iva: **Can the homeowner subdivide in their own name or should they have a separate entity?**

John: If the homeowner wants to subdivide in their own name, that's generally the easier option as the property's probably already in their name. If the property is in a different name, it'd be like a business dealing. So, when they subdivide, there's nothing stopping the homeowner from creating separate entities. But then it's a case of transferring ownership or setting out how the business relationship would work.

Iva: **Is there anything else you'd like to add?**

John: You just need to do your homework. So, when you engage an accountant, financial planner, agent or developer, you check to make sure you're happy with who you're dealing with. Also, look at agreements, engage a legal person to make sure they check out, and make sure you understand what you're engaged in.

In any investment, there's always going to be some risk, but you do what you need to mitigate those risks. And for any professionals you deal with, you need to understand what they're saying to you, rather than just saying, 'Yes, that's good.' You should know why it's good or not good. Look at the detail if you're signing something. There's no point taking a risk without understanding what you're taking a risk for.

The other thing is insurance. Always take out insurance because it's your biggest asset.

AN INTERVIEW WITH LAWYER COLIN ADNO

✕– – – – – – – – – – – – – –

Iva: Colin, please tell us about yourself.

Colin: I qualified as a lawyer in South Africa in 1987, and worked as a property and commercial lawyer in Johannesburg for a number of years. I then moved to New Zealand in 1991, requalified as a lawyer there and worked until 1997, when I moved to Melbourne and began my career here. Once I had requalified in Australia, I started my own law firm called Colin Adno & Associates. Our main focus was property and conveyancing.

More recently, I've merged my firm with Batten Sacks and I'm the property partner. In my specific area, I deal mainly with conveyancing, planning applications, off-the-plan contracts, and anything to do with property. We also advise on property acquisitions and dispositions, subdivision, planning, building, leasing, residential and commercial.

Iva: We are exploring what legal help a person needs in developing their site. How can you help homeowners in this regard?

Colin: I think it's very important that the clients do not skimp on the professionals. It's all very well to try to save money, but that can be more expensive in the long run. It's better to spend money upfront, finding out that the property is wrong for what you want, and walk away from the deal.

So, the homeowners should bring the contract to me on day one, so we can make sure, from a legal perspective, that they're protected. We also work in conjunction with their accountant, planning person or architect to make sure that the whole scenario is going to work.

Iva: **What if the homeowner already has property and wants to subdivide and develop? What kind of service can you provide to them?**

Colin: We check to see if the title is allowed to subdivide. There are properties that have covenants on them where they are not allowed to subdivide, or they might be covenants that have restrictions as to what can be done. We do this in conjunction with a town planner or an architect because there is no substitute for doing research and the due diligence first.

In addition, there can also be planning restrictions that we can assist with ... It might be that the town planner or the architect is more familiar with the planning side, but it all has to be researched and checked.

Iva: **So what are the risks involved in developing?**

Colin: The risks are more commercial and financial, and how much money you spend on the initial investigation and the deal itself. The risks are more about the costs of not doing your budget and your calculations correctly, if I can put it in that way. The other thing that is a risk is that planning schemes and planning laws change. I've had clients who went through the whole process and then the council implemented a new planning strategy.

You also have objections [from neighbours] ... I'm not saying the objections are valid or not, but those kinds of things can delay the planning process by two to three years, and you've got to put everything on hold while it goes through the planning process and possibly even the courts. I tell people they should be very conservative with their planning and always look at the worse-case scenario, and make sure that they can afford to hold the property for a long period of time without getting any return.

Iva: **What about joint ventures? How can you help the home-owner in this situation?**

Colin: With joint ventures, the agreement needs to be done correctly. Every scenario is different and every contract is going to be different. So, the risk involved with the joint venture is that you might use a document that doesn't cover your specific circumstances. And people tend to only really read the agreement if things go wrong. If they do, your agreement has to cover that scenario. So, you have to make sure it's all planned and put down in writing.

The agreement also has to say what each person has to do, how much money they have to put in, and how they share the expenses and the profits at the end.

Iva: What about the builder's contract? Can you help the home-owners with that?

Colin: Most builders use contracts approved by an industry organisation, so there's not much room for negotiation. However, you nearly always have an issue with the builder because there are so many things that can go wrong in a building arrangement. Also, the prime cost (PC) items always seem to be misunderstood. These are the items where the owner has the choice, for example, of how many lights to put in a room. The contract says three lights in the room and you might want ten. Or you want a step coming out of the house into the garage and it doesn't include that. All of those changes add money to the cost, so the PC items can be a problem.

There is also the timeframe. Sometimes builders take a little bit longer than they're supposed to, but they can always adapt the total time allowed because of weather and public holidays and things like that. So, there can be an issue as to time but we can help. For example, we can add in the agreement that there will be a limit on the extra time permitted for weather and holidays. If the builder doesn't comply, they will incur a penalty for every day they're over the limit.

Iva: Do you make sure the builder has proper insurance to protect the homeowner?

Colin: Yes. We check the builder's insurance and warranty insurance. The other thing we advocate is paying the builder on a percentage method. When you pay only at certain times, there is more you can hold back until the end. If you owe the builder a lot of money at the end, they will come and finish the job properly and fix all the defects. But if you owe a very small amount, some builders don't care if they lose this and move on to other projects.

Iva: **Do you have experience with home-and-land package sales?**

Colin: Yes, and there's different kinds of home-and-land [packages]. You either have a separate contract for the land, where you buy the land as a vacant plot and then you engage a builder. That's called a two-part contract, and you have to set up the land and do planning and the build permit work before the builder can start construction. The other way, you buy the land and the building together, which means you're buying it from the developer or they need to get a contract with the builder or they're giving you the complete product. There's no right or wrong way to do it – it's just a commercial calculation.

Iva: **What recommendations do you have for homeowners wanting to subdivide and develop their land?**

Colin: Make sure that your planning people are not pushing the envelope when it comes to requirements or limits. You want to give the council the opportunity to approve the application rather than reject it. All they want to do is help you if your application is within their planning guidelines. So, your planning people should have a meeting with council. It's always better to talk to people before you lodge an application to find out what they want and how they think your application will go through the process. And this sort of thing happens in the due diligence period in the planning process, and should be done with your neighbours and council and your professionals. And then, from the legal perspective, make sure your paperwork is ready to go, so they don't have to wait. Be ready for things when they happen, rather than reacting to them and doing everything in a rush. That's when mistakes happen.

Iva: **When should homeowners looking to subdivide and develop their backyards come to you?**

Colin: In the beginning. We can point them in the direction of people, like a surveyor, and we can take them through the plan of subdivision, processes and lodging. If they are going to be doing a joint venture with someone, then its terms and conditions need to be discussed and put on paper, so everybody understands what each party is doing and putting into the joint venture – be it time, resources or money – and who pays what and how the profit is to be shared. It all needs to be done in advance. The risk is that you spend time and money doing that, and then the joint venture doesn't go ahead. But it's better to spend money on something and let it fail than to go down the path where you've skimped on the legals and find that you have a dispute.

Iva: **I understand lawyers charge either hourly or on a fixed rate. What is your model?**

Colin: It depends on the work we're doing. I try to agree [on] fees in advance, if possible. However, there are certain things where I've got to quote on an hourly rate. For example, for litigation, when I go to court and don't know how long it's going to take. But when it comes to basic things, like conveyancing or agreements, we have a fixed quote for those services. At the end of the day, it has to be done properly and so it shouldn't be all about price.

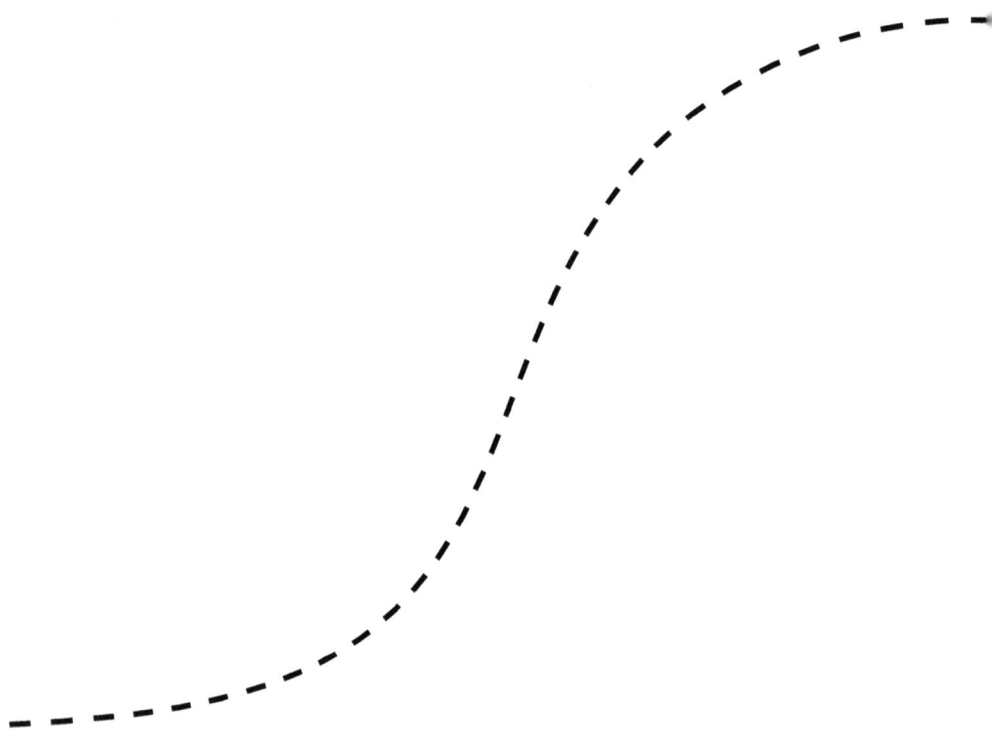

AN INTERVIEW WITH MORTGAGE BROKER LEANNE WATSON

- - - - - - - - - - -X

Iva: Leanne, can you please tell us a little bit about yourself?

Leanne: My name's Leanne, I'm from Your Finance Angels, and we're a boutique broking company based in Melbourne and we have clients all around the country. I've been in broking for sixteen years.

Iva: What do lenders look for from borrowers when they want to subdivide and develop their land?

Leanne: There are basically five things that a lender looks for, and they're all based around the borrower: Who they are and what they do, what sort of credit history they've got, and whether or not they think they're going to be able to get the money back from that particular borrower.

And then it's based around the security – what sort of security is [in the property] and how much equity the borrower has in it.

And then there are times when it's actually based on the economic environment at the time – not just in the local area that they live in but in the state, in the country and globally – as to whether lenders are comfortable lending money to people who want to develop their property.

Iva: **So, does it make any difference if the homeowners have an existing mortgage?**

Leanne: It depends on how high that mortgage is in relation to the value of the property. If there's a very small line [of credit] and the property is worth a [decent] amount of money, then it's going to be a lot easier than if they've just refinanced the property and taken as much as they can get. So, there's got to be enough money left in the property for the lender to be comfortable that if something goes wrong with the development that they can sell it and recoup their money.

Iva: **What is the highest loan [amount] that the lender will lend to homeowners?**

Leanne: It depends whether you're talking the residential space, or whether you're talking commercial space. If you're talking residential space, then it would qualify as a refinance if they're taking money. Even if they've got no debt on their property at all, it's still classified as a refinance because they've already owned that property.

Generally speaking, the maximum loan amount is ninety per cent on a refinance in that space. In a commercial space, it's about sixty-five to seventy per cent. There are some commercial lenders that will lend higher but not for construction.

Iva: **If the homeowners get a residential space refinanced as a home loan, and later on they want to develop, can they then get a construction loan?**

Leanne: It depends on how much equity is left in their property. And the end value of the development that they're going to do.

Iva: **Where do people run into trouble and what can they do to avoid this problem?**

Leanne: A lot of people bank-hop. They go to one bank, they get a no. They go to another bank, get a no. Or they might go to one bank and get offered one loan, and then they decide to shop around. It's not like building a house where you can get three quotes and you take the one in the middle, because every time you go for finance, you get an inquiry on your credit report. Every lender will do a credit check on you to see what sort of credit history you've got of paying your own bills and whether or not you've ever been in trouble before.

You can't knowingly shop around in the lending space because a lender will think that if you've gone to too many different lenders in a short period of time for the same project, there's something wrong with the project. And then more lenders won't want to actually take that project on because you've shopped around too much.

So, if you're doing the legwork yourself to get a mortgage, then potentially, particularly at the moment, you're going to come into strife. Because there are very few lenders that are lending to do property developments at all, particularly in the residential space.

But even in the commercial space, if you've got a project that's less than $10 million, you'll find that there's only one or two offerings in the marketplace at the moment, and there is only one offering that will consider what's called a low-doc loan for a self-employed person. (Low-doc loans are designed to benefit those people who have some existing equity or a deposit saved, and have trouble showing evidence of regular income. This could apply to the self-employed or casual workers. Low-doc loans could also be made available to people with a bad credit history.)

Iva: **So, if the project that the borrower is looking for is a construction one, can you please tell us about the different types of construction loans?**

Leanne: A construction loan either falls in the residential space, which is covered by the National Consumer Credit Protection (NCCP) Act, or the commercial space, which is not governed by the National Consumer Credit Protection Act. If your loan is covered by NCCP, those loans are governed by responsible lending criteria. So, the borrower has to show that they're financially savvy, that they understand what's expected of them, that they can service the loan, and they're young enough to be able to pay that loan back prior to retirement or within a reasonable length of time from the age of retirement. Or else that they have a clear exit strategy for getting out of the loan at the same time as they want to retire.

With a commercial loan, yes, you have to be able to service the loan, but part of that depends on your strategy going forward. If your strategy is to buy and sell, you can capitalise the interest into the loan as you're going along and then you can sell it at the end, and the loan is going to be paid out and you'll make a profit and move on.

If you've got a buy-and-hold strategy, then you really have to make sure that not only can you afford the loan at the start, [but] that you can actually afford the loan at the end as well. And lenders will take a lot more – we want a lot more information about you and your ability to service the loan in that space than they do on a buy-and-sell strategy.

Iva: **And is a construction loan normally interest only?**

Leanne: Generally speaking, for the period of construction, the loan is always interest only. I've never heard of anybody paying principal and interest during construction.

Iva: **You talked about age. I've heard that there are age restrictions on borrowers. Can you please explain that in more detail?**

Leanne: All lenders, for anybody that's fifty or over, all lenders will require an exit strategy from the loan, particularly in the residential space. They need to know that they're not going to be put in a position where they will have to evict anybody because they can't afford the loan. They also want to know that they're going to get their money back as well.

If you've got somebody who's asset-rich and got lots of properties, and you can sell one or two properties to pay back the bulk of the loans, then lenders don't usually have a problem lending to those sorts of people. If you've got somebody who is approaching retirement, has very little money in their superannuation fund, and has only one property that they live in themselves and that's mortgaged to the hilt, then it's going to be a lot more difficult for them to borrow money than for the first scenario.

Iva: What kind of fees can the borrowers expect to pay?

Leanne: Again, that depends on whether it's a residential loan or whether it's a commercial loan. If it's a residential construction loan, it's going to be anywhere from nine to eighteen months long, and you would expect that most brokers would charge you the commission on that.

A lot of brokers will charge a fee for service for a property development loan because there's a lot of extra work in that sort of loan, and they're very hard to get if you go to a bank yourself. So, you probably do need to pay for that experience.

If you've got a commercial loan, there are a lot of fees to be aware of, so you really do have to do your due diligence on your project and understand the feasibility of it ... Lenders will also charge you upfront for the valuation fee, which can be anywhere from $2,000 to $3,000, without any guarantee that you will get the loan. If you've got a sensible mortgage broker, though, then most of that other stuff is worked out before you've actually gotten the valuation. You get a conditional approval subject to the valuation, in most instances.

And then the fees tend to be a percentage of the loan amount. Most lenders will want you to have at least a five per cent contingency. So, whatever your top price is to build, they'll add five per cent to that loan amount in case something goes wrong.

Iva: **What if the homeowner was to borrow money for funding the initial costs of the planning and architectural drawings? Is that something you could help them with?**

Leanne: If they've got enough equity in their home, yes. If they're really well positioned financially, then potentially you might be able to get them an unsecured loan to do that, but again they've got to look at the feasibility, because for an unsecured loan you're paying anywhere from two or three times a home loan rate.

Iva: **How about mortgage brokers versus banks? What is the best path for the borrower to take? And why?**

Leanne: I think if you're a serious investor, then you really do need to have a good team around you. Be that tradies and builders and architects, and that would also include a mortgage broker and accountant. Ten years ago or so, a lot of people who were property investors had a relationship with their bank manager, and often that manager would be able to do things that not even a mortgage broker would have a hope in Hades of doing.

But these days, banks don't leave their bank managers in any location long enough to really build up a relationship with any one particular person. So, you would be very hard struck to find somebody that you could include as part of your team. You might have them there for six months, you might be lucky enough to have them there for two years, but that would be an exception these days. If you've got a good mortgage broker, somebody that you work well with, then that's somebody that you can build a relationship with; that you can talk to about what it is you plan to do.

Because if you're a serious investor, it's not just about this one project. It's about the next project and the next project and the next project, and there are things that you don't consider if you are just doing one. If you get the money for one project, because of the way you've structured the loan, you might not be able to borrow the money for the next project. So, you really do need to have that strategy in place going forward, and you can't do that with a bank person these days because the chances are you might do that with one person and then in six months' time you go back and that person's gone, and then you have to start again.

Iva: **How would you help a borrower obtain finance?**

Leanne: First of all, you have to do a fact find. You have to know who they are and how old they are, and where they live and how long they've lived there, and how they're employed and whether they're self-employed, and how long they've been in that job. You have to have a complete assets and liabilities list of everything they own, and everything they owe. And that's your starting point. Once you've got that, then the next group of questions are all about: What do you want to do going forward? Is this a one-off project and you're going to be happy with that? Or, if this goes well, are you going to do another project?

You're committed down the path of property investing. So, it's all about your goals and, with property development, how you want to move ahead on that sort of thing. Once you've got those bits, all that information, then it's like putting together a jigsaw puzzle where you've got to research the lenders and work out which ones are lending to investors at the moment. There's a whole pile of lenders that are at the point where they are almost unable to lend to investors, and so therefore they have lower loan-to-value ratios and higher interest rates, and higher buffering in the servicing calculators. Then there's those lenders in the marketplace that are still able to lend to investors. Then it just depends on whether you're bringing your own occupied property into the mix or whether it's just the investment property.

Iva: **How does a borrower select a mortgage broker?**

Leanne: Part of it has to be on whether you click; whether you understand each other. If you're asking questions and the answers coming back are not ones that empower you to make better decisions on the information that you're given, then you would probably want to consider looking for somebody else.

What I personally like to do with my clients is empower them to move forward because I think the more understanding and knowledge they have, then the better the decisions they're going to make, the more projects they're going to be able to do, the better it is for them, and the better it is for me. So, it's about working together and finding somebody that you can actually work with, and talk to openly and honestly about the projects that you're considering going forward.

I had one client come to me – he had been knocked back by one lender and, on the face of it, he looked like your dream client as a mortgage broker. Millions of dollars' worth of properties. I did an enormous amount of work and it was just when the APRA, the Australian Prudential Regulation Authority, was coming in with their stuff about investment lending ... I would've got the whole thing over the line if he had just told me the truth about his credit report.

And it wasn't just that one thing. You've got to be able to have confidence that your mortgage broker has got a grip on a large variety of lenders on their panel, so part of that is how many lenders does the mortgage broker have on their panel? Are they restricted to the lenders that are on their aggregator panel? Do they have access to private funding if need be? They're all things that, as a serious property investor, you would need to have a good understanding of in making a decision about choosing a mortgage broker.

The other thing is being aware of the constantly changing environment that is lending at the moment. During the GFC, there started to be some restrictions on low-doc and no-doc lending because they attribute the bulk of the cause of the GFC to those loans in America. Whereas in Australia, the regulations are too strong, even back then, for that to have ever happened. But it did impose some tighter regulations than what we had experienced up until that point.

AN INTERVIEW WITH PROPERTY DEVELOPER AND MENTOR ROB FLUX

✕- - - - - - - - - - - - -

Iva: **Rob, please tell me about yourself.**

Rob: I've been in property my entire adult life. I bought my first house at the age of eighteen with a very creative deal – buying the house that I grew up in from my parents. After doing that I read a book by Jan Somers called Building Wealth through Investment Property, which set me on a journey of buying and holding property. I bought my first investment property at the age of twenty-one, which helped me to own my principle place of residence outright at twenty-four. After this I continued with multiple other buy and hold properties.

After losing much of my wealth at age thirty-seven through a divorce, I decided that I didn't want to wait another twenty years to build my wealth through passive buy and hold with no control over the outcome. So I built on what I already knew and further educate myself on property development so that I could force value onto property in any market through my own sweat equity.

I officially retired several years ago at the age of forty-five by developing property.

During this journey, I also launched a group called the Property Developer Network – it started with a few mates of mine started getting together in my lounge room, then became a Meetup group, and now runs Australia-wide with a range of courses, mentoring and life coaching.

We have also developed our own feasibility software called QwikFeaso to help the developers determine the profitability of projects in minutes. Qwikfeaso is unique in that it has the ability to pre-load common costs into over 20 different development scenarios. So when doing a feaso they simply select which development strategy is appropriate for that site and all the common costs are loaded in seconds. Of course, the accuracy of any feasibility revolves around the site analysis and so we have hundreds of individual line items to use as a check list to ensure that nothing is missed in analysing the deal.

Iva: **What do you recommend for the homeowner thinking about subdividing and developing their backyard?**

Rob: Education is the key to success; ignorance can be very expensive. If you haven't done it before then pay someone who has for their expert advice, do a training course, get a mentor, or find some way of gaining the knowledge from someone more experienced than you. When you're educated, you ask better questions, and with better questions you get better answers.

Iva: **In this book, I recommend the homeowner first goes to the council to find out what can be done on their property. Do you agree?**

Rob: Yes, but that's only the first step. Councils will tell you what rules apply and what generally can be done with the site, but they typically won't commit to an answer on what they will accept. It's a great place to start and it's free, but there are plenty more answers that you will need before deciding to proceed.

Next I would be to engage a private town planner to assess the site for the likelihood of council accepting the application. In my experience, most town planners will typically give you some minimal time assessing the site for free to tell you if you are wasting your time or not.

Beware: Both of these pieces of advice will tell you if you can do it, but neither of them will tell you should you do it. Just because the council will allow you to do what you want to do does not mean that it will be a commercial success. This is where your feasibility becomes critical. In my experience about ninety per cent of sites with development potential do not have the necessary profit potential to justify the risk, but many people naively go into deals that don't make sense only to find out the hard way at the end of the process.

Iva: **So what questions should they ask the town planner?**

Rob: The big one is what constraints they can see on the property. The zoning will only tell you the maximum potential for a site – the constraints are what will limit your ability to achieve this potential.

Some constraints can be resolved, while others may be a complete show stopper. Look for things like location of services, flood or overland flow on the site, protected flora/fauna, contours of the site, soil types, contaminated land, heritage protected building, and so on

Once you understand the constraints, find the relevant expert to talk too to see if the problems can be solved, and if so what the costs will be.

Iva: **When the homeowner wants to apply for a planning permit, how do you help them with this step?**

Rob: Our preferred model is to teach clients how to do it for themselves – how to assess the site, how to do the feasibility, who to engage as experts on your team, how to project manage the process, selecting the right builders, and the like.

We also do joint ventures with some clients where we run the project from start to finish and they are the money partner. This allows us to keep using our expert skills doing what we do best even when our funds are tied up in other deals. It is a win/win for both parties.

Iva: **What are the permits required for subdivision, planning and building? Are there others needed for things like tree removal and exceptions to the regulations?**

Rob: Permits are a very Victorian term. In the rest of Australia and in Queensland where I am from, we refer to them as approvals or development approvals. There are lots of them, but they fall into five general categories with a number of sub categories:

1. **Council**
   Development Approval
   Operational Works Approval
   Earthworks Approval

2. **Utilities**
   Sewer & Water Approval

3. **Building approval**
   Electrical
   Hydraulic
   Structural
   Environmental

4. **Construction certificates**
   Slab
   Framing
   Plumbing
   Electrical

5. **Titles**
   Council - Plan Sealing
   Titles Office – Issue Titles

Iva: **Who are the other professionals needed to carry out the subdividing and developing?**

Rob: You need to have a Core Team of four experts for every development: a town planner, an architect, a civil engineer (sewer, stormwater, water), and a surveyor.

Depending upon the site you may also need additional advice from other experts such as arborists, bushfire consultants, traffic engineers, hydraulic engineers, acoustic engineers, landscape engineers, quantity surveyors, builders, lawyers, accountants and more.

Iva: **Do you have any insight on how to select these professionals?**

Rob: Ensure that the person you are engaging has done this style of project before. It is better to have two consultants who each have a niche specialty than have 1 who is the jack of all trades and master of none.

Iva: **Any horror stories or any success stories you'd like to share?**

Rob: No horror stories, luckily, however my sweetest deal (not my biggest by a long way) was a very basic splitter block that made $190,000 in only a couple of months. Deals like this don't come along every day, but they certainly make your day when they do.

I personally love this deal because when I am teaching newbies to do it themselves it is the perfect example of what can be done part time while still working your regular day job, and the income from it will likely be double what most of them are making each year.

Iva: **Tell us a little about your QwikFeaso software and how it can help with project feasibilities?**

Rob: QwikFeaso is intended perform feasibility calculations and determine construction costs in minutes and not hours or days. It is a highly customised spreadsheet aimed directly at small to medium-sized development projects without the major costs of some of the other larger feasibility software platforms. If you do one of our courses we include it for free, otherwise you can purchase separately through our website at www.developernetwork.com.au

QwikFeaso is based on a three-stage assessment process that we teach in our courses to ensure that you are only spending time in a project that has a high likelihood of success. The three stages are:

1. **Quick assessment:** Uses typical project costs from the pre-saved strategies to assess a site in minutes. The intent here is to not be accurate to the final dollar, but to determine within an order or magnitude if the site has enough potential for profit to justify spending additional time analysing it. The quicker you can throw away bad sites, the more time you have to assess the good ones.

2. **Detailed analysis:** Allows you to manually override the typical costs for site specific variations. This allows you to tweak the initial assessment with the specific issues/opportunities identified for your site.

3. **Due diligence:** Use the hundreds of built in line items of costs as a checklist to ensure that you have captured all the costs on your project. Without a checklist, many people will miss costs within their project. This avoids the situation where the feasibility will look good on paper but the project cannot actually deliver on the profit projected.

Iva: **What are the most important factors in performing a feasibility, and do you teach these in your courses?**

Rob: There are three critical elements in your feasibility – the site analysis, engaging your consultants and completing sales research.

In the site analysis you will identify the issues, constraints and problems to be solved. When you engage your consultants, you can get their expert opinion on what it will cost commercially to resolve those issues identified. And sales research is about determining what the finished product will sell for. Get this wrong and, no matter how perfectly you do steps one and two, the project will never work.

'Wealth is not about having a lot of money;
it's about having a lot of options.'
– Chris Rock

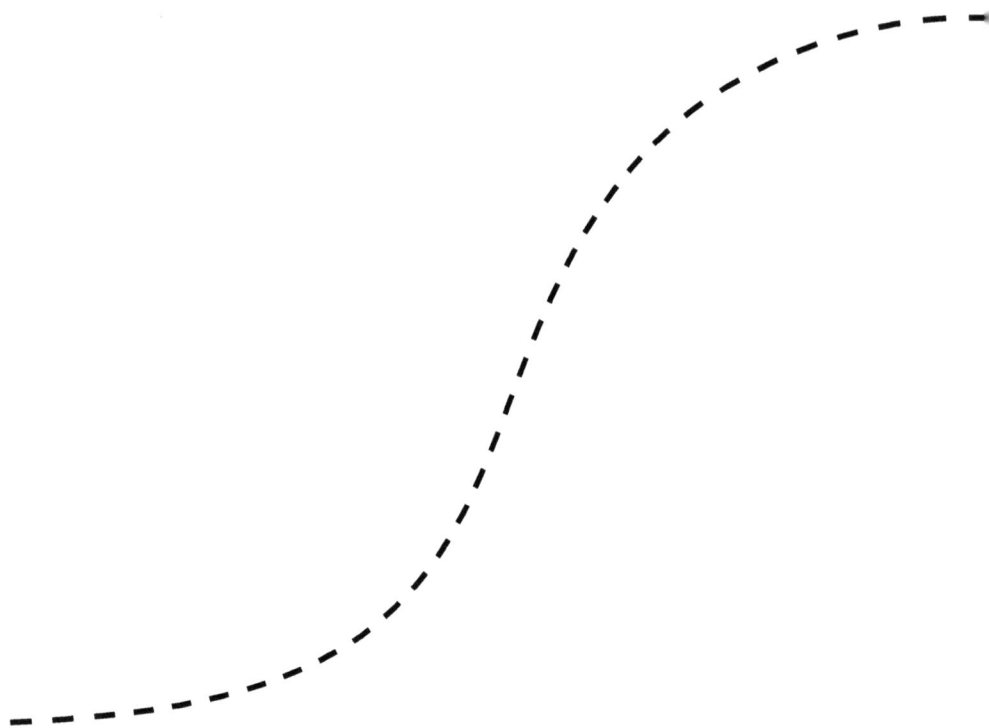

CONCLUSION: BUILDING A PROFITABLE FUTURE

‒ ‒ ‒ ‒ ‒ ‒ ‒ ‒ ‒ ‒ ‒ ✗

While the prospect of subdividing and developing your backyard may seem daunting, I hope this book has given you a solid understanding of the process involved and, more importantly, the confidence to do it yourself in order to unlock the hidden value of your most valuable asset: Your property.

Over the years, I have met many people in your shoes and, quite frankly, felt the task was beyond them. But they have gone on to secure their financial future by following the seven-step guide outlined in this book, and by surrounding themselves with a team of experts to help them.

Things to keep in mind as you proceed along your journey to unlock the cash in your backyard:

1. Educate yourself – learn enough to make an informed decision.

2. You are not expected to, nor should you try to be, the expert in all things, so find the experts and surround yourself with them.

3. Balance the cash to be generated at each potential exit point along your journey with your needs, desires and timing for receipt of that cash. Ask yourself – when is enough, enough?

To recap, here are the seven steps you need to follow:

STEP 1: DEFINE YOUR STRATEGY

Figure out your end goal, determine whether your land is suitable for subdivision and development, learn about your development options, and choose an exit strategy.

STEP 2: GET COUNCIL BUY-IN

Learn everything you can about your council's rules and regulations concerning residential subdivision and development, and strive to get your neighbours on board.

STEP 3: ASSESS YOUR PROJECT'S VIABILITY

Create a concept design, identify and document all of your costs, determine your tax requirements, and calculate your return on investment.

STEP 4: SECURE FUNDING

Secure finance for your project by getting a loan or a line of credit, using your own cash, or forming a joint venture partnership.

STEP 5: APPLYING FOR YOUR PERMITS

Follow the nine-step planning permit process, and speed up the approval process by speaking to your neighbours and council in advance, and including all necessary information in the planning permit application.

STEP 6: WORK WITH YOUR BUILDER

Find a builder suitable for your project, and work closely with them throughout the construction process, from tendering, drawing up a contract, and organising licences and permits, through to site supervision throughout the build.

STEP 7: GO TO MARKET

Find a real estate agent to help you find buyers or tenants for your property, and then present your property so that it attracts the best price.

After you go through all these steps and finally unlock the cash in your backyard, what are you going to do with the money? Pay your mortgage, top up your superannuation, go on a holiday?

Whichever way you decide to spend the money, one thing is clear: Subdividing and developing your property can make a huge difference to your retirement and quality of life.

You may even find that you enjoy the process so much, you'd like to do it again with another property. (It will be a lot easier the second time around, given that you already have the necessary team in place, and are more familiar with the process.)

Whether it's your first time or your tenth time developing property, you can start by giving my team and me a call. We will put you on the right path regarding your property needs.

Every day, my team and I help homeowners around Australia subdivide and develop their properties, and, in turn, achieve their financial and lifestyle goals. If you would like to discuss the specifics of your project and have your questions answered, we would welcome the chance to talk with you and help in any way we can.

'All our dreams can come true,
if we have the courage to pursue them.'
– Walt Disney

You can contact us at www.premierpropertydevelopments.com.au or iva.norris@premierpropertydevelopments.com.au.
Mobile: 0431 099 100

May your dreams become reality!

(Signature)

GLOSSARY OF TERMS

X- - - - - - - - - - - -

Architect: An architect designs and draws up plans for buildings, bridges, and so on, and generally supervises the construction.

Backyard: As used in this book, the backyard is the excess space in your block which may be sufficiently large to build other unit(s). It could actually be in your backyard, your side yard, or your front yard.

Block: This is the land upon which your house is built. It has a unique title. Also used interchangeably with 'lot' and 'parcel'.

Builder: This is the general term for an individual, company or partnership that carries out residential as well as commercial building work. The 'spec' builder (a person or company that builds houses to sell to anyone who will buy them, rather than for a particular customer) is a licensed builder and therefore does not need to contract out the work, but can do their own residential building work.

Owner-builder: An owner-builder is someone who takes responsibility for domestic building work carried out on their own land. They are responsible for obtaining building permits, supervising or undertaking the building work, and ensuring the work meets building regulations and standards. In Victoria, an owner-builder can only build or renovate one house every five years and must intend to live in the house once completed.

Building design: Building design refers to the design of homes, workplaces, public buildings, and so on. It requires a broad skill set, including an understanding of building and construction materials and techniques, business management, specification writing, residential building codes and standards, sustainable building design, and managing project administration.

Buyer's agent: A buyer's agent is enlisted by the buyer to find them a suitable site or home to purchase. The role of the buyer's agent is to find the best possible match for the buyer and negotiate the best possible price. The agent is paid an agreed fee, which is either a fixed fee or a percentage of the total value of the property. Percentage-based fees are typically between one and two per cent, depending on the price of the property.

Conceptual design: This is an early phase of the design process, in which the broad outlines of what you want to build is articulated. Artifacts of conceptual design are concept sketches and models that can be shared with council planners when discussing what is possible on your block of land.

Certificate of Title: A Certificate of Title is a person's record of interests and rights affecting their land. The Certificate of Title is issued by the Registrar of Titles to the person entitled to it, e.g. the registered proprietor or mortgagee. The Certificate of Title shows the date it was created, plus all registrations and recordings made in the Register at the time. This includes the name(s) of registered proprietor(s) and other interests such as mortgages, covenants and caveats.

Depreciation schedule: A list of the depreciable assets related to owning an investment property, including the building itself, so you or your accountant know what deductions to claim.

Developers: Developers buy land, finance real estate deals, and build new properties or engage builders to do so. Ultimately, they orchestrate the process of development from beginning to end. They take the greatest risk (in terms of money outlaid) but are also the ones who stand to reap the greatest rewards.

Door-knocking: A term that refers to an unsolicited approach by a real estate professional directly to the resident at their home. In this book it refers to the author and her team approaching home owners to discuss the possibility of subdivision and development of their block.

Engineering: A structural engineer focuses on the stability and strength of the construction. They ensure that the building comfortably bears the load for which it has been designed, and that it can withstand any natural forces (such as wind, waves and earthquakes, as well as stresses caused by the modern environment, such as traffic). Structural engineers often work with architects, builders and other engineers (mechanical, electrical and chemical) to organise and supervise construction. (to understand about the various types of engineers you may encounter go to "The engineer" in Meet you Team)

Feasibility study: A feasibility study is an analysis of how successfully a project can be completed. Conducting a feasibility study will help to determine the viability of the proposed development by giving an estimate of costs and return on investment. Determining early on that a development will not work saves time, money and heartache later.

Holding costs: The cost of borrowed money. Those funds obtained to pay for the development of your property. They are calculated by multiplying the money borrowed times the interest rate times the length of time from receiving the funds until the loan is repaid.

Laneway: Also referred to as an alleyway. These are normally single lane paved or unpaved passageways behind houses. Not all houses have laneways. They are used to provide access to the rear of a residence.

Line of credit: A line of credit is money made available by a financial institution and backed by equity the buyer has in a property. It can be drawn down or accessed and repaid multiple times, normally without having to re-qualify for the funds as long as your equity in the property is sufficient to support the loan.

Overruns: In this book, overruns are expenses incurred in excess of those originally planned. Time can also be overrun, but seldom without a corresponding budget overrun.

Planning permit: This is a legal document that gives permission to use or develop a particular piece of land. A planning permit usually contains a series of conditions that regulate how the land can be used or developed, and is always subject to a time limit setting out when the planning permit expires. A planning permit is also accompanied by endorsed plans that show what is to be built and how the land can be used. The proposed use or development must satisfy all the conditions on a planning permit, and comply with the endorsed plans. This means the use or the buildings and works must be undertaken as shown on the endorsed plans.

Real estate agents: Real estate agents are the people you deal with face to face when buying or selling property. These are the people on the front lines of the real estate market, and perform such tasks as showing homes to prospective buyers, and negotiating transactions on behalf of their clients. Real estate agents often work on a 100 per cent commission basis, meaning their income is dependent upon their ability to find suitable property for their clients and, ultimately, close transactions.

Real estate development, or property development: This is a multifaceted business process, encompassing activities that range from the renovation and release of existing buildings, to the purchase of raw land and the sale of improved land or parcels to others. Real estate developers are the people and companies who coordinate all of these activities, converting ideas from paper to real property. Real estate development is different from construction, although many developers also manage the construction process.

Renovate/Remodel/Reform: All terms which imply improving an existing home. Councils have specific permitting requirements when it comes to such improvements being made to existing structures, often triggered by the value of the improvement or the extent of the improvement. For example, greater than 50% of the structure being improved may require a permit.

Sales agent: A sales agent represents the seller in their quest to find a buyer for their property, whether that's via private sale or auction.

Subdivision: A legal process of splitting an existing title to a block of land into two or more titles. Requirements for subdivision vary from council to council.

Surveyor: There are three types of surveyors: Land surveyors, building surveyors and quantity surveyors. A land surveyor assesses the layout of the site. This includes measuring and recording the details of the land area. Building surveyors are specially trained to determine the safety of buildings and whether there are any problems with their structure. They deal with legal issues and permits surrounding planning and construction. Quantity surveyors are responsible for keeping an inventory of costs and materials used for construction, and for preparing a depreciation schedule.

Variation: A variation is an exception to a rule, regulation or agreement. Here it is most commonly used as an unplanned change to a set of detailed building plans and specifications for the manner in which those plans and specifications will be built. It is also commonly referred to as a 'Change Order', as the builder will request the developer to agree to a change in the original agreement, and state the change and the additional cost, if any, for implementing the change.

Viability: A measurement of a project's ability to meet your goals. As used in this book it applies to a council's definition of a block of land that meets the requirements for subdivision (the block is a viable candidate for subdivision) as well as financial (the sale of the development will result in a viable return on your investment, permitting you to retire in comfort).

Tender – Is to make a formal written offer to carry out work, supply goods, or buy land, shares, or another asset for a stated fixed price. In the context of a development project, you, the property owner, is asking one or more builders to submit proposals stating how and for what price they will build the units as described in your detailed drawings and specifications.

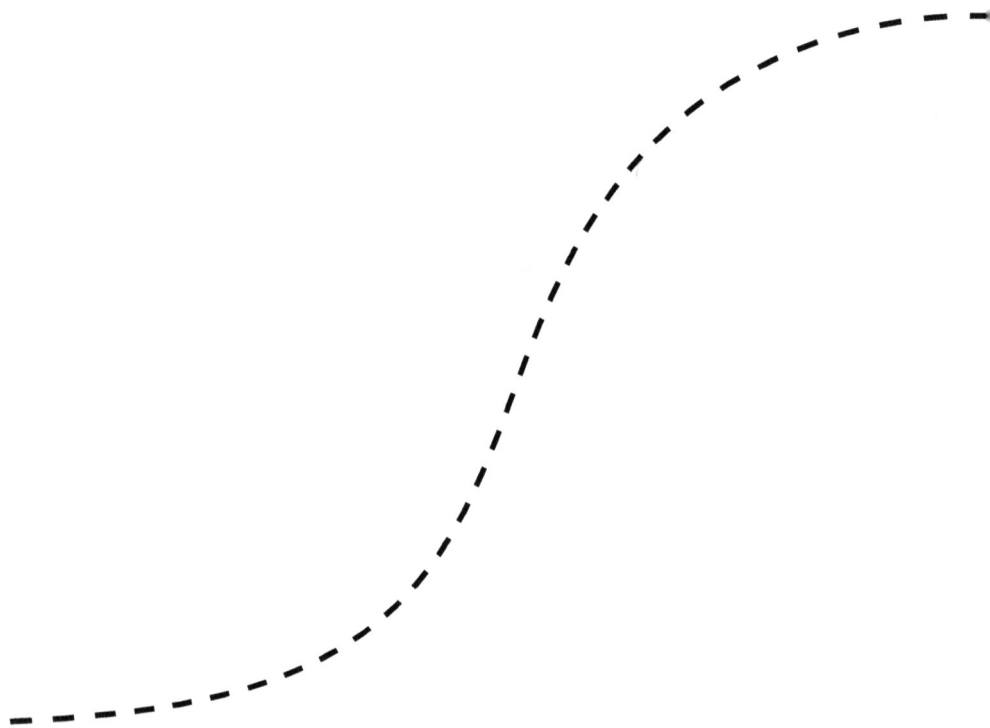

HELPFUL LINKS

As promised, here are some links that may come in handy throughout the subdivision and property development process. The list includes everything from property websites to apps for house paint colours.

Home Sold Price (house.ksou.cn)

This website helps individuals find sold properties, and provides clear and data-rich Information to home buyers. It also provides information to support home-buying decisions.

Domain (www.domain.com.au)

The site offers the latest market intel for buyers, sellers, renters and investors. It also delivers property marketing solutions for new developments, residential and commercial properties. Information about sold properties can be found under the site's 'Sold' section.

Realestate.com.au (www.realestate.com.au)

This property resource site helps people find sold, for sale, and for rent properties through its property listings section. Property developers, home buyers, or anyone looking for a house to rent can find all the information they need, including price, location, size and real estate agents. It also gathers the latest updates on the property market.

Planning Alerts (www.planningalerts.org.au)

This is a free service that enables shared scrutiny of what is being built (and knocked down) in peoples' communities. It also searches as many planning authority websites as it can find, and then emails users the search details.

Houzz (www.houzz.com.au)

This website is a platform for home design and/or remodelling. It also serves as an online community for homeowners and home professionals.

Paint My Place (www.paintmyplace.mobi)

Paint My Place is an iPhone and iPad app, designed for people who want to visualise house paint colours. It can help owners looking to re-model their homes, as well as professionals – painters, realtors, interior decorators and landscape designers – in their development project.

BMT Tax Depreciation Quantity Surveyors (www.bmtqs.com.au)

BMT Tax Depreciation Quantity Surveyors is considered the largest and most successful tax depreciation company in Australia. It specialises in ATO-compliant tax depreciation schedules for residential and commercial investment properties. It has tax depreciation and construction cost calculators, which you can use for your property development project.

Magic Plan app (www.magic-plan.com)

This floor plan creation app is helpful in creating dimensioned floor plans without measurements or drawings. It can also estimate DIY or home improvement costs in a matter of minutes.

SketchUp (www.sketchup.com)

SketchUp is a 3D modelling computer program for a wide range of drawing applications such as architectural, interior design, landscape architecture, civil and mechanical engineering, and film and video game design. The program has paid and free versions.

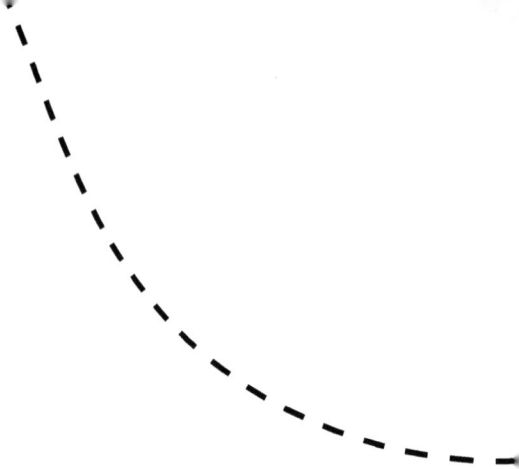

APPENDIX A: EXPANDED FEASIBILITY LIST

-- -- -- -- -- -- --X

LEGAL & ACCOUNTING FEES

Purchase of Property including searches

Creation of Purchasing Entity(s)

Joint Venture Documentation

Drafting of "Off The Plan" Contract

Settlement of "Off the Plan" sales

Body Corporate Setup

Taxation advise and Lodgement

DEVELOPMENT APPROVAL

Town Planner

– Preparation of Application for lodgement

– Post Logement Variations (Hourly Rate)

Council Application Fees

– Pre–Lodgement Meeting

– Reconfiguration of Lot

– Material Change of Use

– Acceleration Application Fee (RiskSmart)

Architect

– Conceptual Design (Schematic Design)

– DA Drawings

– Council Request for Info (Changes to Design)

Civil Engineer

– Code Compliance Report

– Preliminary Earthworks Plan (if required)

– Hydraulic Report for Flooding or Overland Flow (if required)

Surveyor

– Detailed Survey Plan including Natural Ground Level (NGL)

– Detailed Survery Plan

– Pegging of Boundary

– Proposed Subdivision Plan

Advertising of Development

Traffic Engineer

Acoustics Engineer

Landscape Designer

Quantity Surveyor

BUILDING APPROVAL

Architect / Draftsman

– Building Application Drawings

– Construction Documents

Engineering

- Soil Test

- Engineering Design

- Sewer & Water Detailed Design

BA Approval

- Building Certifier

- BERS Energy Compliance

- Hydraulic plan

- Electrical plan

- Plumbing Application & Approvals

- Electric and Telecommunication Agreements

RENOVATIONS & MINOR BUILDING WORKS

Building Works

- Raise / Slide / Restump House / Relocate

- Foundations

- Extension

- Stairs

- Decking

- Windows

- Doors

- Insulation

- Painting

- Plastering

- Rendering

- Roofing
- Carpentry
- Termite Damage
- Asbestos Testing & Removal

Electrical

- Lights
- Fans
- Switchboard upgrade
- Power Points
- Airconditioning
- Solar

Flooring

- Carpets
- Tiles
- Floor Sanding

Plumbing

- Services Connections
- Taps & Sinks
- Hot Water System
- Gas

Kitchen

- Cabinetry
- Appliances
- Taps & Fittings

- Tiling

- Splash Backs

Bathrooms

- Cabinetry

- Appliances

- Taps & Fittings

- Toilet

- Bath

- Tiling

Laundry

- Cabinetry

- Appliances

- Taps & Fittings

- Tiling

Property Staging

- Furniture

- Window Dressings

- Soft Finishes

Landscaping

- Minor Earth Works

- Paving

- Plants

- Soil / Sand / Gravel

- Lawn

Authority Fees

– Insurances

– Application Fees

– Approval & Inspection Fees

House Raise / Slide / Restump / Relocate

– Proposed Plans (Architect / Draftsman / Engineer)

– Building Certifier

– Council Application Fees

– Council Bond (if Required)

– Building & Pest Report

– Pest Treatment

– Roof & Gutter Upgrades (if required) including Cyclone compliance

– Power Connection

– Water Connection

– Sewer Connection

– Gas Connection

– Earthworks

– Additional Height Stumps up to 2.7m (if required)

DEMOLITION

Building Certifier

Gas Abolishment

Power Abolishment

Water Capping

Sewer Capping

Demolition

Temporary Fence Hire

Silt Fencing

Minor Earth Works

Site Clearing

CIVILS

Civil Engineer

 – Detailed Design Documents

 – Tender for Construction

 – Manage construction & compliance to completion

Civil Construction & Operational Works

 – Stormwater

 – Sewerage

 – Water

 – Erosion & Sediment Control (Silt Fencing)

 – As Build Drawings (Surveyor)

Authority Fees

– Utility Service Advice Notice

– Utility Application Fee

– Utility Request Fee

– Utility Engineering Fee

– Council Application Fee

– Council Compliance / Certification Fee

Potential Additional Costs (If Required)

– Location of Sewer & Stormwater Pipes

– CCTV investigation of Sewer & Stormwater

– Stormwater Detention System (Tank / Rubble Pit)

Surveyor (as built documents)

SITE PREPARATION

Minor Earth Works

Clearing of Vegetation

Driveways, Crossovers & Footpaths

Fencing

Landscaping

Retaining Walls

Silt Fence

Temporary Fence Hire

Temporary Toilet Hire

PLAN SEALING & TITLES

Surveyor

– Survey Plan including easements

– Building Format Plan

Easement Documents (If Required)

– Solicitor to prepare "Access Easement" Docs

– Council to prepare "Drainage Easement" Docs

– Utility to prepare "Services Easement" Docs

Compliance Documents

– Telstra Compliance

– Electricity Compliance

– Plumbing Compliance

– Body Corporate

Council

– Plan Sealing Lodgement Fee

– Easement Fee

Titles Office

– Titles Searches

– Titles Lodgement Fee

– Easement Lodgement Fee

MISCELLANEOUS COSTS

Surveyor

– Detailed Survey Plan including Natural Ground Level (NGL)

– Detailed Survery Plan

– Pegging of Boundary

– Proposed Subdivision Plan

HOLDING COSTS

Rates

Water & Sewerage

Electricity

Gas

Land Tax

FINANCE COSTS

Application Fees

Valuations

Quantity Surveyor Report

PROJECT DURATION

Months Holding (prior to Construction)

Months Constructing

Months for Sales

APPENDIX B: UNIT INCLUSIONS, ROOM BY ROOM

PORCH	DESCRIPTION
Lighting	Double LED flood light with sensor
Downlights	1 x 10 watt white integrated flat LED dimmable down light
Double deadlock to front door	
Concrete Slab	Plain finish concrete
Ceiling Lining	Fibre cement sheet
ENTRY	**DESCRIPTION**
Down Lights	White Astro 13W LED CCT dimmable fixed round IP44 illuminati downlight with warm, cool or daylight globe
Ceiling Height Standard	2400mm to ground floor
Ceiling Height 2 Storey Homes	2700mm to ground floor and 2400mm to first floor
Door Type	Hume Newington Vaucluse Premier XVP11, XN1, XN5, XN6, XN7, XN16 clear glazing and painted finish. 2040mm high x 820mm wide

GARAGE	DESCRIPTION
General Description	Garage with tiled hip roof including plaster ceiling, concrete floor and fibre cement infill above garage front door opening. Note: flat roofed garages will have metal deck roof cover in lieu of tiled roof
Single Roller Door	Steel-line panelift colourbond sectional lift up door (Slimline, Glacier, Ranch, Flat Line & Heritage)
Double Roller Door	Steel-line panelift colourbond sectional lift up door (Slimline, Glacier, Ranch, Flat Line & Heritage)
External Entry Door - Garage to outside house (Where provided)	External garage access door 2040mm high flush panel ply door
Internal Entry Door - Garage to inside house (Where provided)	Internal access door 2040mm high hinged redicoat flush panel door
Garage Ceiling	10mm plasterboard
Lighting	2 x diffused double flourescent
Power Points	2 x double white power points Hager slimline silhouette range
Flooring	Plain finish concrete
Ceiling Height	2400mm

MASTER BEDROOM	DESCRIPTION
2 Down Lights (Bedroom)	White Astro 13W LED CCT dimmable fixed round IP44 illuminati downlight
Power Points	2 x double white power points Hager slimline silhouette range
Power Points with USB	1 x double white power point with USB
Windows	Aluminium improved by A & L Windows
Door Type and Size	2040mm high hinged redicoat flush panel door
Flooring	Carpet from Category 2 range
ROBE	DESCRIPTION
Robe	Extent as per plan with single shelf 1650mm high approx. and chrome hanging rail with an aluminium framed vinyl or mirror sliding door & nest of shelves @ 400mm wide
Walk-in Robe Door - Opening or Cavity Sliding	2040mm high hinged redicoat flush panel door
Downlights (WIR)	2 x White Astro 13W LED CCT dimmable fixed round IP44 illuminati downlight with warm, cool or daylight globes
Flooring	Carpet from Category 2 range

MASTER ENSUITE	DESCRIPTION
Frameless Glass Shower Screen	Premium Oz frameless clear glass shower screen with swing door or fixed glass panel only (no door)
Tiles to Shower	Wall tiled to 2 metres high from Category 2 range
Niche to shower wall	300mm high x 500mm wide
Hand Held Shower Head	Jess round rail with 3 function shower head
Wet Area Plaster Board & Pre Tile Waterproofing	
Downlights	2 x White Astro 13W LED CCT dimmable fixed round IP44 illuminati downlight with warm, cool or daylight globes
Power Points	1 x double white power point Hager slimline silhouette range
Stone Vanity Tops	20mm Stone Benchtops in Sparkling White 1210, Platinum Black 1240, Dapple White 1220, Sugar Rush 1270 Crystal 1290, Black Pearl 1190, Mottle Grey 1250, White Burst 1200
Vanity Cupboard	Polytec Cabinets Laminate matte or sheen finish with 200mm high tiled splashback as per plan
White Porcelain Basin	Number as per plan. Refer to list in Internal Fixtures below.

Chrome Taps	Jess pin handle basin mixer
Chrome Toilet Roll Holder	Caroma Enix
Towel Rail - Standard	Caroma Enix
Mirror	Premium Oz polished edge full width above vanity units
Dual Flush White Porcelain Toilet	ECT Qubi II toilet suite or ECT Monarch toilet suite both with soft closing seat
Ceramic Wall Tiles	Western Distributors Category 2 range. As shown on plan.
Ceramic Floor Tiles	Western Distributors Category 2 range. As shown on plan.
Privacy Lock	
Ceiling Exhaust Fan	3 in 1 fan/2 globe heater/light
BEDROOM 2	**DESCRIPTION**
Downlights	2 x White Astro 13W LED CCT fixed round IP44 illuminati downlight with warm, cool or daylight globes
Power Points	2 x double white power points Hager slimline silhouette range
Power Points with USB	1 x double power point with USB
Windows	Aluminium improved by A & L Windows
Door Type and Size	2040mm high hinged redicoat flush panel door

Robe - Standard	Extent as per plan with single shelf 1650 high approx. and chrome hanging rail with an aluminium framed vinyl or mirror sliding door and 4 fixed shelves @ 500mm wide
Walk-in Robe Door - Opening or Cavity Sliding	Painted finish flush panel door
Flooring	Carpet from Category 2 range
BEDROOM 3	**DESCRIPTION**
Downlights	2 x White Astro 13W LED CCT dimmable fixed round IP44 illuminati downlight with warm, cool or daylight globes
Power Points	2 x double white power points Hager slimline silhouette range
Power Points with USB	1 x double power point with USB
Windows	Aluminium improved by A & L Windows
Door Type and Size	2040mm high hinged redicoat flush panel door
Robe - Standard	Extent as per plan with single shelf 1650 high approx. and chrome hanging rail with an aluminium framed vinyl or mirror sliding door and 4 fixed shelves @ 500mm wide
Walk-in Robe Door - Opening or Cavity Sliding	Painted finish flush panel door
Flooring	Carpet from Category 2 range

KITCHEN	DESCRIPTION
Downlights	4 x White Astro 13W LED CCT dimmable fixed round IP44 illuminati downlight with warm, cool or daylight globes
Power Points	3 x benchtop double / Dishwasher x 1 double / Refrigerator x 1 double
Power Points with USB	1 x double power point with USB
Bench Tops	Stone benchtop 20mm Stone Benchtops in Sparkling White 1210, Platinum Black 1240, Dapple White 1220, Sugar Rush 1270 Crystal 1290, Black Pearl 1190, Mottle Grey 1250, White Burst 1200
Kitchen Cabinets (Base and Overhead)	Polytec Kitchen Cabinets Laminate matte or sheen finish. 1 bank of 3 draws with cutlery insert and soft close draw runners
Canopy Range Hood	600mm stainless steel slide out rangehood
Cooktop	Bellissimo 600mm gas cooktop
Electric Fan Forced Oven	Bellissimo 600mm, 62 litre electric fan forced oven
Dishwasher Ready (Dishwasher NOT Included)	Opening will accommodate a 600mm wide dishwasher
Stainless Steel Double Bowl Sink with Drainer	Alpha International Alfa Brisbane 11/2 Bowl

	OR Alpha International Alfa Brisbane double bowl
Chrome Flick Mixer Tap	ECT Jess kitchen sink mixer
Splash-Back (as per plan detail)	Tiles to be 600mm high unless stated otherwise
Soft Closing Doors and Drawers	
Cutlery Drawer with Built in Cutlery Tray	
Windows	Aluminium improved by A & L Windows
Flooring	Tiled
PANTRY (Where Provided)	**DESCRIPTION**
Downlights	1 x White Astro 13W LED CCT dimmable fixed round IP44 illuminati downlight with warm, cool or daylight globes
Power Points	2 x double white power point Hager slimline silhouette range
Shelving	4 x fixed melamine shelves
DINING ROOM	**DESCRIPTION**
Downlights	2 x White Astro 13W LED CCT dimmable fixed round IP44 illuminati downlight with warm, cool or daylight globes
Power Points	2 x double white power point Hager slimline silhouette range
Windows	Aluminium improved by A & L Windows

Door Type and Size	2040mm high hinged redicoat flush panel door
Flooring	Carpet from Category 2 range
LIVING ROOM / LOUNGE / FAMILY	**DESCRIPTION**
Downlights	4 x White Astro 13W LED CCT dimmable fixed round IP44 illuminati downlight with warm, cool or daylight globes
Power Points	3 x double white power points Hager slimline silhouette range
Power Points with USB	1 x double power point with USB
TV Aerial Point	
Windows	Aluminium improved by A & L Windows
Door Type and Size	2040mm high hinged redicoat flush panel door
Flooring	Carpet from Category 2 range
MAIN BATHROOM	**DESCRIPTION**
Bathroom Entry Door	Hume Doors & Timber Hume internal flush panel door 2040mm high
Bath Tub	Caroma Vivas 1675mm bath 71 wide
Bath Spout	Caroma V7703 Spout.
Shower/Shower Taps	ECT Regen shower rail
	ECT Rain jet shower rail

Frameless Glass Shower Screen	Premium Oz frameless clear glass shower screen with swing door or fixed glass panel only (no door)
Shower Base	Insitu or Hebal hob tiled shower base
Tiles to Shower	Wall tiled to 2 metres high from Category 2 range
Niche to shower wall	300mm high x 500mm wide
Hand Held Shower Head	
Wet Area Plaster Board & Pre Tile Waterproofing	
Downlights	2 x White Astro 13W LED CCT dimmable fixed round IP44 illuminati downlight with warm, cool or daylight globes
Power Points	1 x double white power point Hager slimline silhouette range
Deluxe Range Stone Vanity Tops	20mm Stone benchtop in colours Beton 1191, Charcoal Wash 1360, Cimento 1231, Cookie 1350, Fossil 1444, Iron 1340, Kirec 1071, Marvel 1390, Moonstone 1420, Nutmeg 1410, Pearl White 1320, White Truffle 1395
Vanity Cupboard	Polytec Cabinets Laminate matte or sheen finish with 200mm high tiled splashback as per plan
White Porcelain Basin	Number as per plan. Refer to list in Internal Fixtures below.

Chrome Taps - Bath	ECT Jess pin handle bath mixer
Chrome Taps - Basin	ECT basin mixer
Chrome Toilet Roll Holder	Caroma Enix
Towel Rail - Standard	Caroma 600mm Enix single towel rail
Mirror	Premium Oz polished edge full width above vanity units
Ceramic Wall Tiles	Western Distributors Category 2 range. As shown on plan.
Ceramic Floor Tiles	Western Distributors Category 2 range. As shown on plan.
Privacy Lock	
Ceiling Exhaust Fan	3 in 1 fan/2 globe heater/light
TOILET	**DESCRIPTION**
Dual flush white porcelain toilets	ECT Qubi II toilet suite or ECT Monarch toilet suite both with soft closing seat
Ceramic Floor Tiles	Western Distributors Category 2 range. As shown on plan.
LAUNDRY	**DESCRIPTION**
Downlights	1 x White Astro 13W LED CCT dimmable fixed round IP44 illuminati downlight with warm, cool or daylight globes
External Sensor Light (Where external door supplied)	

Power Points	2 x Double white power point Hager slimline silhouette range
External Door (Where required)	Aluminium sliding door or Hume XF3 painted and clear glazed door with aluminium window to one side
Door Type and Size (Where required)	Hume ply door 2040mm high
Flooring	Tiles
Taps	ECT Jess laundry sink mixer
Trough	ECT Lavassa stainless steel laundry trough 45 litre
	Alfa 45 metal laundry trough
Splash-back Tiled	As shown on plan
Washing Machine Connections	Washing machine stops mounted in cupboard Caroma (Nogging support for dryer)
Towel Ring	Caroma Enix
Bench Tops (as per plan)	Laminex from Builders choice
Cupboards (as per plan)	Polytec Cabinets Laminate matte or sheen finish with 200mm high tiled splashback as per plan
ALFRESCO (Where included)	**DESCRIPTION**
Power Point	External power point
Ceiling Fan	3 speed

OTHER INCLUSIONS

PRELIMINARY	DESCRIPTION
Obligation Free Site Appraisal	
Fixed Price Contract	
Soil Report	IF SHOWN IN QUOTE
Engineer Designed Slab	IF SHOWN IN QUOTE
Working Drawings	IF SHOWN IN QUOTE
Electrical Layout Drawings	IF SHOWN IN QUOTE
Building Permit Application & Fees	IF SHOWN IN QUOTE
Public Liability Insurance	Insurance for all contractors working on site
Builders Insurance	
Energy Rating Assessment	IF SHOWN IN QUOTE

WARRANTY	DESCRIPTION
180 Day Maintenace Warranty	
10 Year Structural Guarantee	
12 Month Manufacturers Warranty	Rangehood, Hotplate, Oven, Hot Water Service, Solar Unit
SITE WORKS AND ALLOWANCES	DESCRIPTION
Foundations/Fall of Land	Class 'M' Concrete Slab with maximum 600mm site cut
Temporary Fencing & Portable Toilet	As required

Roof Safety Rail	As required
Scaffolding	As required
Termite Treatment	As required
Silt Protection	As required
Waste Bin/Cage	
DOORS, LOCKS, HANDLES	**DESCRIPTION**
Main Entrance Door	Hume Newington XN6, XN7, XN16 clear glazing and painted finish
Rear Garage Door	Weatherproof ply door (where required)
Alfresco / Patio	Aluminium sliding door with key lock
Laundry Door	Aluminium sliding door with key lock or Hume XF3 timber door (where required)
External Front Door Lock	Lockwood Nexion front door lock
External Door Locks	Lockwood District or Vacinity door handles
Internal Door Handles & Locks	Velocity 63mm Internal door handles in satin or polished chrome
Garage Door/s with Two Handsets and Wall Mounted Opener	Steel Line Garage Doors Slim Line, Glacier, Ranch, Flatline, Heritage
Flyscreens to all Sliding Doors	
Quality Sliding Doors	A&L Windows & Doors Aluminium in a range of colours
Door Stops	To all internal and external swinging doors

Kitchen and Vanity Handles	Selected from Category 2 range
WINDOWS	**DESCRIPTION**
Quality Sliding Windows	A&L Windows & Doors Aluminium in White, Surfmist, Merino, Dune, Jasper, Precious Silver, Woodland Grey, Monument, Black
PAINT	**DESCRIPTION**
Three Coat Paint System Throughout - Walls and Ceilings	Haymes Newlife Paints First Coat Prep Ultraseal Undercoat, Top Coat x 2 in Ultra Premium Interior Expressions Low Sheen Acrylic Low BOC
Doors, Skirting & Architraves in Gloss Paint	Haymes Ultra Premium Ultra Seal, Top Coat Newlife High Gloss Enamel
External Grade Paint	Where required
CONNECTIONS	**DESCRIPTION**
Underground Electricity Mains Connected to Main Switchboard	
Telephone Point with Connection Allowance	
Gas Connection up to 20 metres	
PLUMBING AND DRAINAGE	**DESCRIPTION**
Garden Taps at Front and Rear of Property	Standard garden tap
Connection to Mains Water Supply	
Sewer Line	As specified on plan

Stormwater	As specified on plan
Large Capacity Solar Hot Water System	Chromagen single or double solar system / continuous flow hot water booster only
INSULATION	**DESCRIPTION**
Ceiling	Bradford Insulation Refer to Energy Rating Report for R Rating
External Walls	Bradford Insulation Refer to Energy Rating Report for R Rating
EXTERNAL FIXTURES	**DESCRIPTION**
Bricks	Austral Bricks Homestead Redgum, Blackwood, Buff, Access Ash, Access Fawn, Settlers Mannagum, Access Parchment, Harvest Buckwheat
Concrete Roof Tiles 230 Pitch	Bristile Roofing Classic Range - Mulga, Choc Royale, Char Grey, Gun Metal, Charcoal, Shadow
	Bristile Roofing Prestige Range - Palladium, Titanium, Tungsten, Carbon, Carbide
Colourbond Metal Fascia, Gutter and Downpipes	Colourbond Surfmist, Evening Haze, Classic Cream, Paperbark, Shale Grey, Dune, Cove, Pale Eucalypt, Woodland Grey, Windspray, Gully, Mangrove, Deep Ocean, Cottage Green, Wallaby, Jasper, Basalt, Manor Red, Night Sky, Ironstone, Terrain, Monument

INTERNAL FIXTURES	DESCRIPTION
Cornice	75mm cove cornice
Skirting and Architraves	Hume 67 x 18 MDF architraves and skirting
Door Handles & Locks	Velocity 63mm internal door handles in satin or polished chrome
Light Switches	Hager Visage white light switches
Power Points	Visage white power point throughout
	Cyber Range power point to kitchen splashback only
Smoke Detectors Direct Wired to Main Power	
Basin (Select from range)	ECT Lois (Insert Basin)
	ECT Como (Semi Recessed)
	ECT Guarda (Semi Recessed)
	ECT Sorrento (Above Counter)
	ECT Artistic (Above Counter)
	ECT Odessy (Above Counter)
	ECT Picasso (Above Counter)
	ECT Massimo (Above Counter)
	ECT Viola (Above Counter)
	ECT Eternal (Above Counter)
	ECT Vivo (Above Counter)

HEATING	DESCRIPTION
Ducted Heating	Braemar Heating to 8 points
OTHER	**DESCRIPTION**
Wall Framing	MGP10 pine framing throughout
Internal & External	Professional builders clean pre handover
Site Visits	3 x scheduled site visits
Timber Flooring	Where shown on plan. Bordeaux 8mm laminate
Skirting Tiles to Wet Areas	100mm high skirting tiles
STAIRCASE - DOUBLE STOREY HOME ONLY	**DESCRIPTION**
Maple Timber Handrail and Newel Post with Clear Finish	Gowling Stairs MDF staircase carpet finish with timber hand rail mounted to wall if applicable OR as stated on plan

Provided by Timothy Trickey – Golden Key Constructions Pty Ltd

ACKNOWLEDGEMENTS

I would like to thank, first of all, God, for the opportunity to share with the world my vision and my passion for property and burning desire to help others.

When I started my book-writing journey on property development in Australia, it was daunting. The amount of information I had to assimilate was incredible, but I was determined to provide the best possible information to those who could truly benefit from it. Those who aided me along the way included professionals in the industry who gave freely of their time and knowledge – for all those I give a huge thank you! After a gestation period of more than two years with the help of those industry professionals and a great publisher it lives!

I especially want to thank my family for their support throughout this writing journey. And to my friends and business partners who went out of their way to help me with the book and remained friends in spite of my absences during deadlines – a warm embrace, I am back and available once again!

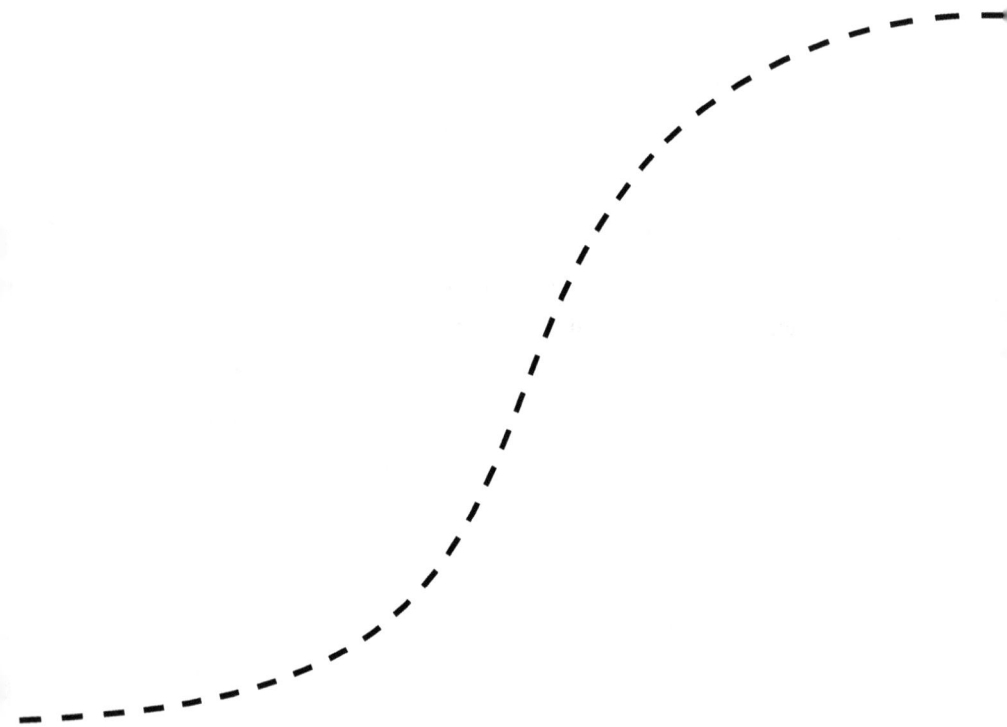

ABOUT THE AUTHOR

Iva Norris has a bachelor degree in Economics and has been an active participant in the international real estate market for over fifteen years, making her first property investment in 2002. She is the founder of Premier Property Developments, which specialises in local real estate investments and developments in Australia, as well as the former owner of three Century 21 agencies in Brazil.

Iva's professional specialities include vendor finance, property development, buying and selling local and overseas commercial and residential real estate.

Iva is Brazilian/American and is fluent in English, Spanish and Portuguese. She lives in Melbourne, Australia, with her husband and the youngest of four children. In her spare time, she enjoys spending time with her family, exercising, reading and attending personal-development seminars.

www.ingramcontent.com/pod-product-compliance
Lightning Source LLC
Chambersburg PA
CBHW060332220326
41598CB00023B/2688